MEN & ANGER

A RELAPSE PREVENTION GUIDE TO UNDERSTANDING AND MANAGING YOUR ANGER

D1256673

MURRAY CULLEN, MA &
ROBERT E. FREEMAN-LONGO, MRC

THE SAFER SOCIETY PRESS ● PO BOX 340 ● BRANDON, VERMONT 05733

LIBRARY OF CONGRESS CATALOG CARD NUMBER: 94-067491

DESIGN: Barbara Poeter

EDITOR: Euan Bear

TYPESETTING: Amy Rothstein

PRINTED BY: Whitman Communications Group, Inc.

ORDER FROM:
The Safer Society Press
P.O. Box 340
Brandon, Vermont 05733-0340
(802) 247-3132

$15.00 each, includes shipping and handling.
Bulk order discounts available.

ISBN: 1-884444-12-1

Acknowledgments

The authors and publisher extend our heartfelt thanks to the learned, experienced, and busy professionals who use Relapse Prevention throughout their work and who took the time to read and comment on this book. They include: G. Alan Marlatt, the father of Relapse Prevention, and his colleague George A. Parks; Richard Laws; Kraig Libstag; Richard Kishur; Jim Mann; and a professional who prefers to remain anonymous.

Murray Cullen offers his appreciation to Marc Brideau, Sandy Piekarski, and the staff at CFC St. John, New Brunswick, for promoting an atmosphere conducive to program and treatment development.

Contents

Figures

Introduction
How To Use This Book

Thank you for purchasing *Men & Anger: A Relapse Prevention Guide to Understanding & Managing Your Anger*. We are pleased that you have chosen to work on your anger as part of your personal program of recovery. Anger is unavoidable. All people experience anger in their lives. You are reading this because you are in treatment for another issue or you are recognizing that anger has become a problem affecting your life. Perhaps you have been broken the law out of anger. Or you may have an abusive pattern that is fueled by your anger and has gotten you into trouble.

As you begin to explore your anger through using this book, we encourage you to keep a couple of things in mind. First, remember that if you have assaulted someone, what you did (your behavior) is terrible—but *you* are *not* terrible! You *can* change your behavior! Second, remember that emotions are not good or bad, including anger. It is what you *do* with emotions that either causes you (and others) problems or helps you live a full life. Your anger can work for you or it can work against you.

This book covers some very difficult topics, and you may feel pretty uncomfortable as you read through this material. Keep in mind that the end result will be positive, worth any discomfort you might feel along the way.

Anger alone is not the problem, the problem is how you deal with it. How you deal with it can run the gamut from healthy expression and constructive action through screaming and yelling, throwing things, to destroying property and hurting people. Some of these behaviors may be chargeable criminal offenses.

Many criminal offenses, especially assaults, begin with feelings of anger and revenge. These feelings are often directly linked to a strong desire to demonstrate control over another person, your victim. Using offensive or criminal behavior to express or relieve emotions usually creates feelings of guilt, shame, frustration, and embarrassment. These feelings often lead to more anger, another offense, more feelings of guilt, shame, and embarrassment, more anger, and on and on in a cycle that continues to feed on itself—*unless you intervene to stop it!* Whether or not you have committed a legal offense in response to your anger, you likely have other ways of acting out toward other people that create feelings of guilt, shame, frustration, and embarrassment within you and that feed into your anger cycle.

You can apply the principles of Relapse Prevention and anger management that you will learn in this book to your personal program of recovery, or not. It is up to you to decide, just as you decide whether to use a hammer to drive a nail, or a wrench. The right tool makes all the difference. We encourage you whenever possible to work on these issues in a specialized anger management program or with a treatment professional experienced in treating people with anger problems. If you must work on your own without professional guidance, we encourage you to discuss your efforts and share what you are doing with a family member or friend who is someone you can trust and who knows about your anger problem.

As you work through this book, you may come across words or terms you are not familiar with. We encourage you to look them up first in the glossary at the end of the book, or, if you do not find them there, look in a dictionary.

Finally, we know from experience with hundreds of men with anger problems that it is very important for you to complete all the exercises at the end of each chapter. The only way you can change this behavior is by observing your patterns of thoughts, feelings, and behaviors, understanding your cycles, learning the skills, and practicing new responses. Doing the exercises helps you understand your anger and learn what to do to control it. A good way to get these homework exercises done is to set aside a few specific times each week—perhaps after your religious services, and Tuesday after supper. If you are trying to stay away from alcohol and bars as part of your program, use some of the time you would have spent hanging out in the local tavern to do your homework. The most important thing is to get into a routine.

We recommend that you keep a journal during this whole process: use a spiral bound notebook for completing your exercises and writing down your thoughts, feelings, and behaviors. Keeping all of your exercises in the same place will help you review when they build on previous assignments, and they can easily be given to your teacher, group leader, or counselor.

We acknowledge and appreciate your effort to work towards a safer society by working to make yourself a safer person. We wish you good luck in your work with your anger and your recovery.

Murray Cullen
CFC ST. JOHN
NEW BRUNSWICK
CANADA

Robert E. Freeman-Longo
SAFER SOCIETY PROGRAM
BRANDON, VERMONT
USA

Chapter One
Working On My Anger

Reasons For Wanting To Change

There are many reasons to participate in a treatment program or to actively work on helping yourself when professional help is not available. You are reading this book because you are making a decision to change your life. Maybe you are tired of feeling angry all the time. Maybe someone has recommended that you read this book because the person believes you have a problem that needs to be addressed. Whether you are in prison, on parole, or on probation, whether you are involved with the legal system or the correctional system, or whether you are afraid that you will be in court or in jail soon because of your out-of-control behavior, you have a reason for reading this book.

Some people you know may support your being in treatment and getting help with your anger; others who don't have faith in you may tell you that there is nothing that will help you. Regardless of what anyone else thinks, the bottom line is that *you* must want to help *yourself*. Once you have made that decision, sticking to your treatment program will be easier if you hang out or socialize with people who support your treatment and your choice to change.

You are probably reading this book because you have noticed that you have one or two key problems or because others have noticed and identified them for you. One problem may be that you have committed a criminal offense, resulting in your being involved with the legal and/or correctional system. Or it may be that you have physically hurt someone close to you, or are in danger of losing your job. Your out-of-control anger harms others. Committing an offense and harming others with out-of-control anger are two good reasons for wanting to change.

One of the most important reasons for wanting to work on managing your anger is to prevent yourself from hurting others in the future. If you have assaulted someone you have hurt your victim(s) in ways that may never be obvious to you. If you have had a problem with your anger, over the years your words and/or actions have caused pain or hurt to many other people in your life. If you have been carrying around a lot of anger for a long time, you may not recognize *how* you have hurt others, *how many* people you have hurt, or even that you have hurt *anyone* at all. We hope that one reason you are motivated to get help with your anger problems is to stop hurting others.

Another good reason for wanting to work on your anger is to spare your immediate family (spouse and children) or other family (including your parents, brothers, and/or sisters) any further embarrassment, shame, or bad feelings they experienced because of your behavior. Your children may be called names in school; your extended family of uncles and aunts may feel shame and guilt they don't deserve because of your public displays of anger.

A third good reason for wanting to change is so *you* can feel better. By carrying around your anger you are probably hurting yourself through constant stress, ulcers, chronic muscle tension, high blood pressure, and headaches. Anger also creates mental pain in terms of frustration, hurt, resentment, etc. Ultimately, angry people push family and friends away. Anger can lead to your feeling bad about yourself.

You may have your own reasons for wanting to learn how to manage your anger.

Although you cannot change the past, you can make positive changes for the present and for the future. Many angry people who become offenders go through treatment, return to the community, and make significant, positive changes in their lives. Some have become involved with service groups and donate their time for charitable causes. Others talk to local groups, identifying themselves as offenders and explaining how treatment has helped them change and make restitution to their victims. These opportunities for community and individual restitution are additional reasons for wanting to change.

Keep your reasons for wanting help in mind while you read and work through this workbook and your treatment. You will find your treatment difficult at times. Making changes in your behavior, thoughts, and emotions is not easy. Below, men in a treatment program who also have anger problems have listed some of their reasons for wanting help with their anger:

- To learn self control
- To understand myself
- To address my problem areas
- To decrease my anger
- To feel better about myself
- To stop my lying
- To develop trust with others
- To correct my wrong thinking patterns
- To learn to manage my stress
- To learn to communicate better with others
- To learn to be assertive with others
- To develop empathy and compassion for others
- To overcome my major fears
- To work out my problems
- To stop undesirable behaviors
- To learn how to understand others
- To help lower my defenses and receive the help I need
- To think about how I affect others around me
- To accept my limitations and weak spots

And the list goes on. What is your most important reason or motive for wanting help with managing your anger in nonhurtful ways?

Change works best when a person *wants* to change. Forcing or pushing someone who does not want to change is usually a waste of time for the client and for the person trying to help him. Help *is* available for you *if* you want help and will continue to work on your anger.

Why Should I Work On My Anger?

Anger can work for you and against you. As you will learn in Chapter Three, anger is neither good or bad—it's what you *do* with it that makes it either positive or negative, healthy or destructive. If your anger had worked for you in healthy ways, you would probably not be reading this book. Since your anger has worked against you in unhealthy ways, then you need to work at changing it before it continues to affect your life in ways that are harmful.

Sometimes your anger has *felt* good, even when you were using it in destructive ways. Other times, feeling angry has felt bad. Some people get confused when they try to understand how something can feel both good and bad at the same time. Many people, for example, don't understand how they can love someone (feelings that feel good) and at the same time feel anger or hatred toward the same person (feelings that hurt or feel bad). If you were abused by a parent you might feel love for that parent (feelings that feel good) as well as anger about what he or she did to you. You may even *hate* the things they did to you (feelings that feel bad or hurt you). Anger itself can often cover up deeper feelings that feel good or bad.

For some people, anger works for them and against them at the same time because they believe that their anger has served a purpose—protecting them (working for them)—even though the end result of that protection has been to push others away (working against them). For example, think about being teased by someone and wanting him to stop. If you put the feeling of anger into behavior and beat the person up (acting out anger), it would stop the teasing behavior (anger working for you). But in addition, a person you like most of the time (except when he's teasing you unfairly) may never come around you again. If others saw you beat up the teaser, they might feel afraid that you would get angry and beat them up. They might also decide not to spend time with you any more (anger working against you).

Responding angrily to teasing is an example of how anger can work for you (stopping the teasing behavior) and against you (pushing other friends away) at the same time. The issue is how to prevent and/or deal with this confusing experience and make things work out right. One solution is to stop the teasing but not push others away who care about you. This requires an understanding of your anger and knowledge of how to intervene in and express angry feelings without acting out your anger in hurtful ways. This is called being *assertive*. When you don't understand your anger and you act it out, others are offended by it and do not want to be around you. Al's situation is a good example.

In the long run, your anger works against you when you *act out* your anger, using it for hurtful or *negative anger action*. When you *manage* your anger by taking *positive anger action*, your anger works for you. We will talk about *positive anger action* later in this book.

Al always wanted things to be his way. When things did not go his way he immediately became angry. For instance, Al thought no one else in the office should ever use the scissors, tape, stapler, paper clip holder, or correction fluid from the table near his desk. His friends at work knew they were for everyone in the area to share and use.

When one of Al's office mates borrowed a stapler, Al got angry. He stood in the middle of the office and yelled, "WHO STOLE MY STAPLER?!"

Trask answered quietly, "I borrowed it for a minute—I'll give it right back."

Al screamed, "You thief! You keep your grubby hands off my desk supplies!" He snatched the stapler out of Trask's hand and stalked over to his desk fuming with rage.

Eventually, Al's office mates—Trask, Jordan, and Bart—stopped inviting him to have lunch together or play basketball after work because there was no room for disagreement without having a screaming match. They began to spend less time around Al. Soon, Al found himself without any friends.

One way that you may be negatively acting out your anger is by sexually abusing another person, either by forcing sex on your wife or girlfriend (rape), or by sexually abusing a child. Sexual abuse is a result of many problems, and one of them is misplaced anger. Initially it seems to work *for* you by making you feel better (a very temporary good feeling). But then it works *against* you (causing harm to another person, prompting feelings of shame, guilt, embarrassment, fear of getting caught, etc.). Many sex offenders commit their offenses because they are angry. Sexual abuse becomes a way of expressing frustration and anger at a person or at a situation. In other words, the anger is expressed through the sexually abusive act. In either case, the anger works for you (release) and against you (fear, guilt, shame, being arrested) and is hurtful to others.

When your anger works against you as much or more than it works for you, you have good reason and need to work on your anger. When your anger results in hurting others, feeling bad, feeling shame, guilt, embarrassment, etc., it is time to make changes in your life.

Chapter One Exercises

EXERCISE #1-1: Why Try to Change?

In your notebook, write down all of the reasons you can think of why you want treatment. You may include some of the reasons listed on page 15 that apply to you, but make sure to add your own personal reasons as well.

EXERCISE #1-2: What I've Done When I Was Angry

Make a list in your notebook of what you have done (behaviors) when you were angry. Go over the list and put a plus sign (+) next to any that you think were positive anger actions. Put a minus sign (−) next to any that you think were hurtful or negative anger actions.

EXERCISE #1-3: How Anger Has Worked For Me and Against Me

List some examples of how your anger has worked for you and against you in your life. Example, anger working for you: firmly telling (not screaming at) the mechanic that he did not repair your car properly and you want the situation corrected; after being confronted, he corrects his mistake at no charge. Example, anger working against you: hitting your wife as a means of releasing frustration; you feel bad about your behavior because you have hurt and scared someone you love.

What Is Anger?

Anger is a feeling. People have many feelings: joy, sadness, guilt, happiness, jealousy, calm, sorrow, excitement, relief, and so on. Anger is one of many feelings we experience. Like other feelings, you can feel a *little bit* angry, or you can feel intense anger, even rage. Feelings are an energy source within you. Energy is *movement*. Normally, your emotions move or flow freely from inside you to the outside world and back again. In other words, when you feel happy, you share that by expressing your happiness. You smile and laugh, play, hug your friends, greet your neighbors. When you have problems and feel depressed you might talk with someone you trust who will listen to your problem. Ideally, your feelings flow and others experience them with you (see Figure 1, next page).

Sometimes people learn to "stuff" their feelings as a way of trying to control the feelings when they become intense. *Stuffing* anger is not the same as *controlling* or *managing* it. Stuffing anger is holding it in, squishing it down inside you, shutting down emotionally, and pretending that you're really not angry. When anger becomes intense, stuffing makes it worse. You begin to lose control of it, and your feeling of anger begins to control you. Your anger may leak out in indirect ways, such as in sarcastic remarks or small anger outbursts at people who don't deserve it. Eventually, the pressure builds up and you explode. This is especially likely when you feel fear and anger together (look again at Figure 1).

Anger is also a *physical* reaction to emotions of fear and threat. When something happens that you perceive as a threat, your adrenaline gets pumping. Your body gets ready to fight or to run. Your

Figure 1
Stuffed Feelings

Normal emotional flow is like having the oil system on your car working well: everything keeps moving through the system. When part of the system breaks down or the filter gets clogged, oil stops moving through the system, and the engine overheats and might be damaged by the grit. Stuffed feelings are like having a broken oil pump or a clogged filter. When your feelings don't circulate, you get emotionally "over heated", and damage to yourself and to others results.

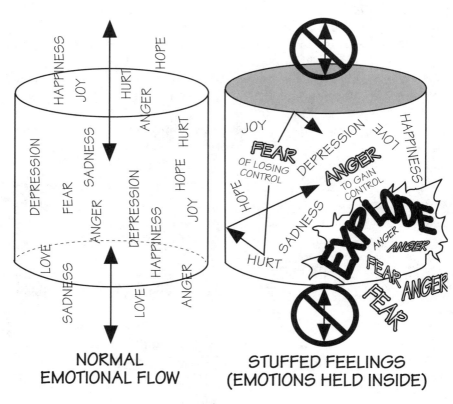

NORMAL EMOTIONAL FLOW

STUFFED FEELINGS (EMOTIONS HELD INSIDE)

face flushes red from extra blood pumping through; or you may go pale when your body directs the blood toward the large muscles in your arms and legs. You breathe fast to get extra oxygen to your muscles. You may feel as though you are watching yourself through the wrong end of a telescope; or you may have never felt so alive and strong as when you are angry and acting out your anger with violent behavior.

Usually the situation that makes you angry is not actually life-threatening. But because your emotions tell your body that this is a life-threatening situation, your body reacts as if you are in real danger. One key to changing the level of your anger is to change your thinking and feeling that a situation is life-threatening to perceiving and accepting the reality that the situation is *not* life-threatening, so that your body does not physically react with preparations for fight or flight.

Some men get angry because they believe that's what *men do*. They think acting out their rage using violent behavior is *macho*, or makes them more of a man. When you realize that most anger is based on fear, it begins to be harder and harder to believe that anger has anything to do with being more of a man. Some men are so scared of having feelings that they cover up those feelings by being angry. Real men, men who are strong within themselves, aren't afraid of having other feelings besides anger.

When you experience fear, you usually feel (fear) that you are losing control. You may fear that you will be rejected by somebody, that you will begin to relive old feelings of hurt and pain that you have stuffed and tried to forget about for years, that someone is setting you up (feeling vulnerable), that your feelings or actions are too risky, etc. As a result of feeling fear (feeling like you are losing control) you may become angry. You may use your anger in an attempt to gain control.

When you respond to fear with anger (to gain control) your anger usually comes out in destructive ways: "acting in" or "acting out." "Acting in" is turning your anger against yourself by doing things that will hurt you (engaging in self-destructive behaviors), such as setting yourself up to fail, abusing alcohol or drugs, and attempting suicide. Abusing yourself by using alcohol and drugs is an attempt to "self-medicate," or to feel less of the pain you experience from being angry. Brian's situation is a case in point.

Brian has an ulcer, probably from stuffing his anger over the years. When Brian gets upset he drinks, even though his doctor has warned him that drinking with an ulcer could land him in the hospital. He just wants to feel that warmth going down his throat, with the old reliable numbness coming after it. He doesn't feel scared or angry when he's had a few double shots, and he likes it that way.

Last Friday, after Brian had an argument with his boss, he went down to Jake's, his regular hangout on his way home from work. On good days, he drinks tonic water and watches sports on the big overhead screen. But on bad days, like this one, he starts guzzling shots.

He knew he shouldn't drink but he was really pissed off. "Damn doctors can't tell *me* what to do!" he thought to himself.

After 3 or 4 doubles Brian suddenly bent over, his face gone deathly pale. Before anyone could even ask what was wrong, Brian vomited blood all over the bar, the floor, and his own pant legs and shoes. His ulcer had begun to bleed and he ended up in the emergency room.

Brian's drinking is a form of "acting in," a way of being angry that is self-destructive. His father had also hit the liquor bottle when he was angry—that's where Brian learned it. But Brian does have a choice, and if he wants to live much longer, he's going to need to learn some new ways to be angry that don't hurt so much.

The other destructive way of expressing anger is "acting out." You may act out the anger you have towards people by hitting them, verbally or physically assaulting them, or sexually abusing them. You may attempt to express your anger toward another person by damaging property—theirs, your own, or even property that belongs to an innocent bystander. Ben had an angry outburst one night that included all three kinds of property damage (his story is on the next page).

Yet another way of expressing anger destructively is pushing others away by harsh words or angry gestures. Calling people names, threatening them, making a fist or pointing a finger in someone's face, and so on, are behaviors that usually intimidate people and push them away.

Many people do not know how to deal with anger. Strong emotions such as anger do not just "go away." Unresolved anger stays with you—it keeps building up inside you when you stuff it. No matter how hard you fight to ignore your anger, it is a battle you will ultimately lose.

Sometimes you may find yourself starting to feel "numb" to the pains of life or to the anger that you feel. This numbing—when you feel like stone or steel—helps you not feel your anger, but it also blocks your ability to feel other feelings, such as happiness and pleasure. Numbing doesn't mean that your anger has gone away, just that you don't feel it for a while. Bottling up angry feelings is a way of becoming violent to yourself because it causes you emotional and physical discomfort, actual pain. Brian has an ulcer, and Ben's hands and feet are all cut up. Michael, another man with anger problems, gets blinding headaches, and Ollie's jaw is sore from grinding his teeth at night. All these physical pains are caused by anger.

Ben was angry at Ralph because Ralph's dog was never tied up, always left turds in Ben's yard, and knocked over his aluminum garbage cans in the middle of the night.

Last week, Ben woke up to the sound of his garbage cans falling over—for the third time that week. Ben went into a rage. He stormed outside in his shorts, picked up a garbage can in each hand, and stalked over to Ralph's backyard.

He set one can down, picked up the other with both hands and threw it through Ralph's garage window. He tripped over the other garbage can, then kicked it halfway across the yard, scattering trash in its wake. He stomped after it, then jumped on it with both feet, smashing it flat.

As Ben stalked back across the yards towards home, his foot came down on a wine bottle that had fallen out of the trash. Ben fell like a tree and lay there a second, stunned, the breath nearly knocked out of him. Then he bellowed with rage, stood up, grabbed the still-rolling wine bottle, and heaved it as hard as he could across the street, where it smashed through the window of the ground floor apartment.

Ben threw open his front door, denting the wall behind it, then slammed it closed again so hard that the window pane next to the door cracked. He was trying unsuccessfully to go back to sleep when the sirens and flashing lights came to a stop on the street in front of his house.

How Did I Get My Anger?

You (like all people) are born with the potential to experience a range of emotions. How you go about experiencing these feelings, expressing them, and coping with them, however, is learned by watching how others do it. Your parents, relatives, friends, teachers, and others were *role models* for your emotional self. How you got your anger can probably be traced to your early learning experiences. When you are young, your role models are older children and adults. You learn to imitate (copy) their behaviors because you look up to them. You learn whatever these people model, whether they demonstrate positive or negative behaviors (or some of both), as in the examples below:

• If you were raised in an environment where your parents *discussed* situations that made them angry, and how to respond to those situations, you would have learned to talk about your anger and come up with ways to resolve the problems causing the anger.

• If you saw your parents yell, curse, and hit the wall or kick furniture when they were angry, you learned to respond to anger the same way, by yelling obscenities and beating up the furniture.

• If you saw your parents hit each other and call each other names when they were angry, you might be doing the same thing with your wife, woman friend, or partner.

• If you were beaten as a child for doing things your parents thought were bad, you may be beating your children.

• If your brother or sister used to pick on you when angry and/or in trouble, you might have learned to take your anger out on others.

The Cycle of Abuse

The anger you have a problem with today may have started when you were a child, especially if you were abused. Physical, psychological, and sexual abuse affect a victim in different ways.

The one thing that all these forms of abuse have in common, however, is that the abuse *never* leaves the victim feeling okay about what happened. Abuse leaves the victim feeling angry (among other feelings) about being abused, taken advantage of, or controlled. If you can remember how you felt when that was done to you, you can begin to understand how your children might have felt if you have acted out your anger with physical or sexual abuse.

If you were the victim of abuse while you were a child or teenager, the abuse you experienced is likely to be one of the *precursors* of your anger. A *precursor* is something that happened before your present problem and affected how you deal with it. Being abused, however, is never an excuse for aggressive or violent behavior. You are responsible for how you deal with the anger you experience today. By reading this book and doing the assignments, you are making the choice to do something responsible about the anger you feel now.

People who were abused and have carried the anger for many years often approach the world from a *victim stance*. They blame others for their problems rather than looking for solutions or making changes in themselves. No matter what they have done to destroy property or hurt other people, they always try to make it look like *they* are the ones who are being harmed. People who remain in a victim stance tend not to get better (healthy) and their problems continue or get worse. People in a victim stance use anger to try to control other people, and when it doesn't work, they decide more anger might do the trick. Carlos's situation (on the next page) shows how someone in a victim stance looks at the world.

Victims who work through their abuse become *survivors*. Survivors no longer let the abuse they experienced control their lives. They know that they can change, work on their problems, and make better lives for themselves. Although most people who are abusive to others were abused themselves, *most victims do not become abusers*. Victims who don't abuse usually had someone to talk to about their feelings, even when they couldn't talk about the abuse itself. This fact shows that you can change, you have a choice about how you want to be. Changing starts with understanding your anger and your behavior, and eventually talking about your feelings.

Carlos was raised in an abusive household. His father beat him with a belt when he broke any rules, and his mother hit him and told him that he was worthless and no good.

Carlos continues to be angry now that he is an adult. He thinks people are "out to get him." He blames others for his problems and gives up when things don't go his way.

When his car broke down, Carlos blamed it on rich car company executives, even though it was Carlos who didn't check or change the oil when recommended, and even drove the car dry. "It'll never be any different," he thought. "Those guys don't care about the people who drive their cars! They only want us to change the oil that often so the dealer can make money off us."

At the same time, way inside where no one could see how he felt, he was feeling stupid about not taking better care of his car. He thought, "Maybe my mother was right, maybe I *am* worthless. I can't even keep my own car running."

He didn't want to feel so bad, so he got angry instead. He drove down to the car dealer's and threatened the manager. "You sold me a lemon! Your bloodsucking salespeople are ripping off us poor working guys! Either you give me a new engine, or all your profits will just go up in smoke. You owe me an engine. You sold me a bad car. It's your fault."

Remaining in a victim stance lets you continue to blame others for "making" you angry. Blame feeds into your anger; it is how kids relate (until they learn better), not how a responsible adult deals with problems. Blaming others gives them power and control over your life. When you take responsibility for what you think, feel, and do, *you* take control of your life. To take control of your life, you have to take a close look at yourself and consider how you learned to express your anger.

The repeated pattern of being abused, stuffing your feelings, and then abusing others is a *cycle of abuse* that unfortunately is very common. Cycles of behavior repeat themselves. In Chapter Six you will learn more about cycles of behavior. Unless you *intervene*, the cycle of abuse continues and your abusive behavior patterns are passed on from one generation to the next, from the abuser to the victim.

If you were abused, it may be that you learned to stuff your feelings, especially your anger, until the anger builds to uncontrollable levels. At that point you may explode and act in your anger on yourself or act out your anger on others. You *learned* these behaviors. You can't exactly "unlearn" them, but you can learn new, healthy, less hurtful ways to deal with your anger. Making these changes, however, means putting in time and effort. They don't happen automatically, even when you mentally "get it" and understand what needs to be done. To change your violent behavior you need to "get it" emotionally, and take responsibility for your actions, your feelings, and the adjustments you need to make.

Controlling Feelings vs. Stuffing Feelings

There are times in your life that you simply would not want to act on your emotions. You know in your mind and your guts that a situation is not fair—for example, when you get laid off from your job. You feel angry or embarrassed, but you know it would be better not to do anything because you might not get called back to work if you confronted your supervisor or acted out your anger. You decide to—and do—*control* your feelings. When your boss yells at you in front of your coworkers for something that you did wrong, you may realize that what he is telling you is true, but you still feel embarrassed and angry about being yelled at in front of others. Again, you feel the need to *control* your feelings by keeping them inside *until you can deal with them later or talk about the experience* that angered you.

Controlling your anger and how you express it is different from *stuffing* feelings. When you *stuff* feelings, you bury them and pretend that they don't exist or that they don't affect you. Maybe once in a hundred times, you may need to *control* your feelings for your own safety or job security. But 99 percent of the time, you need to let your feelings move through you by *asserting* yourself *appropriately*. You can let other people know when you feel pain, guilt, shame, rejection, happiness, and other feelings.

Stuffing feelings is like filling a pressure cooker full of food, sealing the top, blocking the pressure-release valve, and turning on the heat. The more heat, the more the pressure builds. With the pressure-release valve blocked, there's no place for the steam to go, and the kettle blows its top—explodes—even when the heat stays the same. But when the pressure release valve is working, a little bit of steam escapes every second, and you end up with a delicious meal instead of a kitchen disaster (check out Figure 2 on page 25).

Compare this pressure cooker example to feelings you experience and the thoughts you tell yourself about them. Your feelings are like the water in the pressure cooker. You experience feelings such as joy, hurt, anger, sadness, sorrow, fear, happiness, and depression. When you are healthy, you freely discuss your feelings with others (steam escaping little by little through the pressure-release valve). When you stuff your feelings (block the pressure-release valve), you keep them trapped inside. Trapped feelings build the pressure higher and higher. When your feelings are trapped, you begin feeling out of control. Feeling out of control does not feel good. When you feel out of control, you begin to experience fear and anger as a result (remember Figure 1). When you feel out of control is when you try hardest to convince yourself that you are in control and are most likely to act out violently to regain control.

When you experience fear, you become less likely to take emotional risks. You may feel vulnerable, helpless, rejected, and in emotional pain. You feel hurt. All of these feelings are connected with losing control. In some cases, you may feel like a victim of circumstance.

Another result of stuffed feelings is anger. When you feel out of control you are likely to try to gain control at any cost. You might start pushing others away with violent words or actions, or abuse yourself by overdoing alcohol or using drugs, or by spending all of your money without first paying the bills. When your anger builds up and you act out (the pressure cooker blowing up), you might take your anger out on people who do not deserve it, such as friends, co-workers, and/or family members. Denzel had that pressure-cooker feeling often, but especially at work.

If you have assaulted others, you probably stuffed all of your feelings *except* anger just before you committed your assault(s). You probably still practice stuffing your feelings. In order to change, you must begin taking emotional risks. You must put your trust in the people who are willing to help you so that they in turn can learn to trust you. Be aware that your feelings can get the best of you, especially because you probably have a hard time being honest both with yourself and with others.

Denzel wasn't ever quite sure that he was good enough or competent enough at work. He held in his feelings of insecurity and never talked about them with anyone. Denzel's self-esteem became so low, he suspected that others were after his job. When his co-workers came to him with a question, Denzel responded impatiently and angrily and created arguments.

Because Denzel was having a lot of arguments with co-workers, his supervisor put him on 60-day probation and told him he could lose his job if he continued to argue with other staff. Denzel's anger at work continued to build up. Soon he was going home with a full head of steam locked up inside.

As soon as he walked in the door, his rage exploded. He screamed at his wife, Billie, just for telling him that supper would be ready in 10 minutes. His kids Malcolm and Jasmine ran away from this angry monster who looked like their daddy but acted much worse. They hid in the back bedroom under the bed because they were so scared.

In order to change you must take the risk of being honest with yourself and others. When you feel hurt, tell others about it; when you feel upset or angry, let others know. This is another important step towards getting healthy.

Remember the 4 P's of anger:

1. Your anger has a PAST—when you learned hurtful ways of dealing with angry feelings.

2. Your anger has a PURPOSE—what you use your anger for.

3. Your anger has a PATTERN—what you think, feel, and do over and over in response to the same kinds of situations.

4. And your anger has a PAYOFF—what you get by being angry and acting it out.

You can't change the past, but you can learn from it and take responsibility for the present in learning how to use your anger in new, nondestructive ways. You do that by *observing* and *recognizing* the repeating pattern or cycle of your anger and learning to intervene in it. You can discover new ways to do what you want to do (purpose) or change what you want to do. You can get more rewarding payoffs from nonabusive ways of interacting with the world. The rest of this book is about looking at the pattern (cycle) of your anger and how you can change it.

Be honest with yourself as you answer the questions in this workbook. Keep in mind that it is your anger that caused the problems that you are now faced with. It is your anger that hurt your victim(s). It is your anger that led to shame and embarrassment for your family. Wanting to stay out of trouble and to prevent yourself from hurting other people are good reasons to work on your anger and complete this workbook.

Chapter Two Exercises

EXERCISE #2-1: The Four P's

In your notebook, write down the answers to the following questions:

PAST:
1. Who was the angriest member of your family?
2. How did she or he express that anger?
3. Who got hurt?
4. What got broken?
5. When was the first time you remember feeling really angry?
6. How did you express it?
7. What happened then?
8. Compare how you express anger with the patterns of the people you grew up with. Give examples.

PURPOSE:
What do you use your anger for? (Examples: to give me an excuse to get drunk; to intimidate people when I feel crummy) List as many purposes for your anger as you can.

PATTERN:
In your notebook make a chart like the one on the next page— you'll probably want to make the spaces bigger so you can put in more details. During this week, list at least 5 situations where you have gotten angry. For each situation, list the time of day and the day of the week (example: 8pm/Thursday), where you were (at home; in a bar), who or what was involved (wife, boss, parole officer; broken down car, slippery sidewalk), what happened just before you got angry, and what you did afterwards.

MY ANGER PATTERN

	Time/Day	Where	Who Was Involved	What Happened Before	What I Did After
1.					
2.					
3.					
4.					
5.					

PAYOFF:

What do you get by being angry? List at least 5 emotional or physical payoffs. Explain whether you think the payoff is worth it and why.

EXERCISE #2-2: Stuffed Feelings

List the "stuffed" feelings that you experience just before acting out your anger violently. As with the other exercises, make sure you only write down things that are important to *you*!

Anger's Good & Bad Effects

The Good & The Bad That Can Be Ugly

So far, we have talked about anger's negative effect on your life and on the people around you. Anger itself is neither bad nor good—it's what you *do* with it that counts. There are many situations where your expression of anger might be justified. Being pushed or shoved, or being called names, is inappropriate behavior and can leave you feeling angry. Anger can also work for you and help you solve problems. The following are some of the good points about anger:

1. Anger gives you energy. If you are in danger, anger can provide you with the extra "boost" or "energy" you need to escape from a dangerous situation.

2. Anger helps you talk with others. By talking to others, you can avoid feeling increasing tension from your anger building up (like a pressure cooker). When your feelings flow freely, there is less likelihood of your building up hurtful feelings.

3. Anger gives you information. When you feel angry, it is an indication that something is wrong. It serves as a signal to start looking around and finding out why you feel the way you do and/or why you are having problems.

4. Anger can motivate you to take control of your life. It is good to feel that you are in control of your life and the situations in which you find yourself. When you feel out of control you are more likely to experience feelings like fear, rejection, failure, etc. When you try to control others it is a sign that you are losing control of yourself.

5. Anger can motivate you to take action toward resolving a problem. Taking constructive action to resolve a problem helps you feel competent and in control of yourself instead of helpless and victimized.

As you can see from these examples, anger *can* be helpful. Whether your anger is helpful or harmful depends on how you use or express it. People do not need to take their anger out on each other unnecessarily. Unfortunately, many people in our society have problems with their anger. When you ignore your angry feelings and let them build up, you become like a pressure cooker and suffer from the negative effects of anger (see Figure 2).

Some of the *negative* effects of anger include:

1. Anger stops you from thinking, feeling, and acting clearly. When you are angry you may "see red"—you do not think clearly before you act. You do not make good choices. When you are angry you are likely to do things that you later wish you hadn't done. Anger creates "tunnel vision," which limits your ability to see other solutions.

2. You probably become angry more often than you have to. You may become angry whenever you are feeling embarrassed. When you are embarrassed, you may react by insulting or hurting others because your pride is hurt. Instead of admitting you made a mistake and taking the embarrassment in stride, you may lash out at people physically and/or verbally.

3. Anger and aggression have a lot to do with each other. Even though it is okay to feel angry at appropriate times, excessive anger can build up. When you do not take care of your anger, it can lead to aggression.

Remember that anger is a feeling, like joy, happiness, jealousy, and so on. Aggression, however, is completely different. Aggression is taking action against a person, an animal, or an object. Aggression is either physical or verbal. It is meant to cause pain or hurt the object of your aggression. When you are angry for a long time, you

Figure 2
A Pressure Cooker

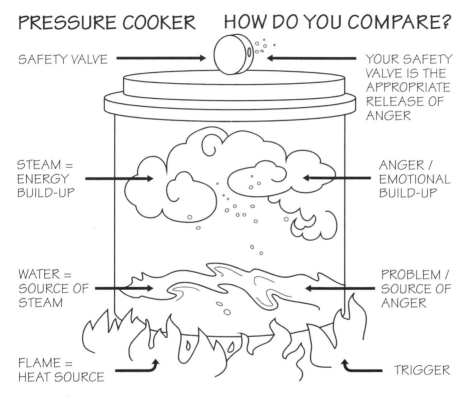

PRESSURE COOKER   HOW DO YOU COMPARE?

SAFETY VALVE →

YOUR SAFETY VALVE IS THE APPROPRIATE RELEASE OF ANGER

STEAM = ENERGY BUILD-UP →

ANGER / EMOTIONAL BUILD-UP

WATER = SOURCE OF STEAM →

PROBLEM / SOURCE OF ANGER

FLAME = HEAT SOURCE

TRIGGER

A pressure cooker builds up energy in the form of steam / heat. The steam / heat cooks the food inside. The safety valve releases extra pressure so the pressure cooker doesn't explode. Your anger works in a similar way. When you build up a lot of anger (energy) and don't have a safety valve (an appropriate way to release your anger) your anger builds, creating more and more energy, until you explode in a destructive anger outburst.

Anger's Good and Bad Effects

are more likely to become aggressive. Your aggression hurts others as well as yourself. All too often aggression results in violence.

4. When you become angry, people think of you differently. When you hold on to your anger for long periods of time and over many situations, people relate to you as grouchy, possibly threatening, somebody who is not pleasant to be around.

People will not trust you. They fear you may lash out at them either verbally or physically. Because you are angry, you feel bad and you may start to insult others as a result of your anger. When you feel bad or very angry, you may push or strike others physically: you commit an assault. The result can be that you do not feel good about yourself.

Few people like to be around people who are angry most of the time. Angry people usually have few friends, mostly other people who have anger problems. Angry people feed into each other's anger. Misery loves company, but the company makes you miserable. Few people want to be around someone who may be verbally and/or physically abusive over even minor disagreements.

Anger is best dealt with at the time you feel it. If you feel angry about something you have choices. You can discuss it with the other person, or you can let the anger build up inside of you until it becomes *aggression.*

Some people's anger grows until they explode into aggressive acts. They lose control and they punch someone, call others names, lash out blindly, break things, rape, molest, scream and yell, kick pets, or knife or shoot another person. Some of these examples, though extreme, happen on a daily basis. In most cases, the victim of the aggression was simply in the wrong place at the wrong time. The victim of aggression does not provoke the angry act. The angry aggressive person may not have even been mad at the victim of the outburst—the angry attacker simply chose to let himself lose control. Eddie's anger problem (next page) demonstrates this point.

In some cases the victim and the attacker do not even know each other (for example in a riot or a mob scene). The person with the anger problem chooses to let himself lose all control. This was the case with Frank.

When anger builds and goes untreated, it can affect your life and the lives of others in a variety of ways. Uncontrolled anger never affects your life in a positive way. It eats away at you like a cancer.

Reading this book and honestly doing the exercises will help you focus on developing your self-control. It concentrates on teaching you the skills you need in order to take control over your own life. Becoming angry and being aggressive and hurtful to others is not being in control. When you are aggressive and assaultive to others, you are *out* of control. It is as if you were a puppet on a string being manipulated by another person or a situation. The person or situation pulling your strings does not really have control over your life. Only you are in control and only you can give others control to pull your strings.

Eddie was home one evening when he had an argument with his wife, Alice. Arguments are nothing new in their relationship, but recently Eddie has begun shoving and hitting Alice when they argue. Eddie has continued to let his anger grow toward his wife and other women. One evening, after a big argument, Eddie went out and drove around to try to cool down. He saw a woman hitch-hiking and picked her up. Eddie propositioned her for sex, and the woman said no. Within minutes Eddie drove to a secluded area, beat and raped the woman. As he left her, he said, "You women are all alike. It's about time someone taught you a lesson!"

Frank was angry most of the time. He often went down to Sully's Tavern, thinking that a drink would make him feel better. Wednesday night at Sully's, another guy bumped into him by accident. Frank snarled, "Watch where you're going, butthead!" and pushed the guy. The guy pushed him back. In a flash of anger, Frank began swinging his fists at the guy and broke his nose. Frank sobered up in the local jail and was charged with assault.

Anger's Good and Bad Effects

Chapter Three Exercises

EXERCISE #3-1: Productive Anger

In your notebook, write down examples from your life when anger has been useful and worked in your favor. Give details: why were you angry? who was involved? what did you do? what happened as a result?

EXERCISE #3-2: Harmful Anger

Write down at least 5 examples from your life when your anger has been harmful to you and worked against you, resulting in harm to others and/or objects. Give details.

Learning to Track and Manage My Anger

Anger management is possible, even for you. Managing your anger is not magic, but a skill you can learn. Before you can learn anger management skills, you need to decide to accept that you have an anger problem. Then you need to want to do something to correct your problem. Finally, you need to make a commitment to stick with the process, even when it feels uncomfortable. In order to begin working on your anger there are some basic tasks you must do, and you cannot take shortcuts. First—and most important—you must become more aware of your anger: 1) what angers you; 2) how you *feel* when you become angry; 3) what you *think* when you become angry, and 4) what you *do* when you are angry. One way to begin increasing your awareness is through **Situation Perception Training** and keeping an anger log/journal.

Situation Perception Training

Situation Perception Training (SPT) is a process for learning anger management. SPT is learning to "think before you act" or "looking before you leap." To understand SPT and the concepts it is based on, refer to Figure 3 on the next page.

Activating events are what happens in the world around us. Activating events can be something you feel, hear, or see. Any of your senses can bring information from an activating event to your brain. Once the information reaches your brain, your brain perceives or *interprets* it and the information is considered a possible *trigger*.

Figure 3
Reacting Or Responding

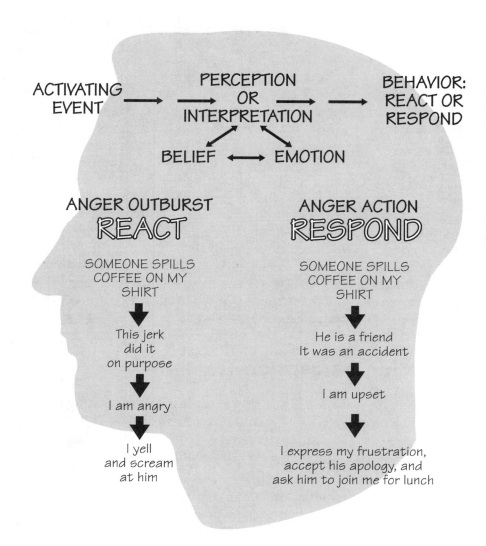

ACTIVATING EVENT → → PERCEPTION OR INTERPRETATION → → → BEHAVIOR: REACT OR RESPOND

BELIEF ←→ EMOTION

ANGER OUTBURST
REACT

SOMEONE SPILLS COFFEE ON MY SHIRT

⬇

This jerk did it on purpose

⬇

I am angry

⬇

I yell and scream at him

ANGER ACTION
RESPOND

SOMEONE SPILLS COFFEE ON MY SHIRT

⬇

He is a friend It was an accident

⬇

I am upset

⬇

I express my frustration, accept his apology, and ask him to join me for lunch

©1994, Murray Cullen & Robert E. Freeman-Longo

Your interpretation is based on your *beliefs* (or what you are thinking at the time) plus the *emotions* you are experiencing. Once you have *interpreted* the trigger situation, you *react* or *respond*. If you have an anger problem, the result can be an acting-out of your anger in an angry reaction or outburst.

It is important to note that an activating event or *trigger* can lead to many different behaviors (reactions or responses). How you interpret the situation depends on several factors. Look at Lance's situation for example.

> Lance was sitting in a cafeteria. Another man, who just served himself and was returning to his table, walked by Lance, accidentally tripped, and spilled hot coffee all over Lance's brand new shirt. Lance stood up in a rage, yelling and screaming at the other person: "You're a stupid idiot! You did it on purpose!" The man tried to apologize and pay for having the shirt cleaned, but Lance, who was furious, told him to get lost.

In this case, the coffee spilling on Lance is the activating event or trigger. Lance can feel the coffee spilling on him and immediately feels the hot wetness on his shirt and lap. He is frustrated and angry that his new shirt is stained and that he was scalded, and he *reacts* in a fit of anger.

This situation could be perceived or interpreted in a number of ways. If the person is someone Lance did not like, he might interpret the trigger event through his belief that the man did not like him and spilled coffee on him on purpose. Lance may even think to himself, "That jerk! He did that on purpose! He is trying to make me look bad in front of the others! I'll fix him!"

As you can see from this example of *self-talk* (Lance's inner thoughts), the emotional value Lance attached to this incident is one of anger. The resulting behavior is likely to lead to a confrontation, including verbal insults. It might get worse, if the other man doesn't accept Lance's verbal abuse, with the possible result that Lance ends up starting a fist fight.

Now let's look at this same situation with slightly different players: the person spilling coffee on Lance is his best friend.

One change in this scenario results in a totally different interpretation. As a result, Lance's behavior is also different. Instead of getting angry, he is upset because his new shirt is stained. He cleans himself off and expresses his frustration, thinking, "Damn! And it's a new shirt, too!" Then he invites Mark to join him for lunch. Even with the same activating event or trigger (the feeling of hot coffee burning him and seeing coffee stains on his new shirt) Lance realizes that the person is his friend. Lance's perception or interpretation this time includes the belief that the person is a friend, and therefore it must have been an accident.

> Lance was sitting in a cafeteria. Mark, (Lance's closest friend) who had just served himself and was returning to his table, walked by Lance, accidentally tripped, and spilled hot coffee all over Lance's brand new shirt. Lance was shocked, frustrated, and upset, but quickly realized that Mark just tripped—it was an accident that could have happened to anyone. Lance was bummed out about his new shirt, but said, "Well, Mark, after that entrance, the least you can do is join me for lunch." Mark apologized for messing up Lance's shirt and offered to get it cleaned. They sat together enjoying their lunch and talking.

The triggering event and damage to Lance's clothes are the same. Lance still feels the same emotions: frustration, and concern about being burned with hot coffee and his shirt being stained. However, because it was Lance's friend, Lance's response to the accident, being burned, and having his shirt stained is changed, and his anger is minimal.

No matter what the situation, what is most important is how you interpret the event. The way you interpret events determines how you will react or respond. Your interpretations are based on what you are thinking at the time and how you are feeling. At times you may "jump the gun" and automatically give a negative interpretation to events. When you do this, you are more likely to become angry and react or act out in a negative or destructive way.

If you find yourself automatically interpreting events negatively, you can change your behavior. When you look before you leap to a negative conclusion, you can often avoid ugly situations from happening at all. One way to increase your awareness and learn to recognize the patterns of anger you have is through keeping a log or journal.

Keeping An Anger Log

In reading about SPT you learned that when events occur, you *interpret* what happened based on your experience. Certain events can *trigger* your anger cycle depending on how you interpret them. As a result of your interpretation of the event, you experience various thoughts and feelings, leading you to engage in certain behaviors. Your behavior does not "just happen." *You* behave in a particular way as a result of the *decisions you make*. You decide to react with angry, aggressive behavior when you interpret events and choose to react to them with anger.

To manage your anger, you must first learn to be more aware of it by keeping track of your thoughts, feelings, and actions. The best way for you to do that is to keep a log or journal of what is happening in your life. A written record gives you the power to know what you think, feel, and do from one day to the next. The most powerful way to use your log is to chart (write down) your behavior every day, especially at the time you experience your anger.

People keep anger logs so they can track where, when, and under what circumstances they *act in* (with behaviors that hurt themselves) or *act out* (become physically or verbally aggressive). Appendix A at the end of this workbook is a single anger log sheet. Make as many copies of a larger version of the blank anger log as you need. You should fill out at least one of these logs every day. Figures 4A and 4B show sample anger logs and how they should be filled out. If you cannot fill out an anger log sheet every time you get angry, keep a small note pad or sheet of paper in your pocket along with a pencil or pen. Every time you get angry, write down a couple of notes about your anger and then fill out an anger log sheet in the evening when you have more time.

Learning to Track and Manage My Anger

As you continue to chart your anger, you will collect enough anger log sheets to begin seeing patterns both in the situations that trigger your anger and in how you react. You will also begin to recognize common patterns of thoughts, feelings, and behaviors you experience when you are getting angry. The greater your awareness, the better the information you will collect about yourself.

When you look back and read your anger log later on, you can see how some of your reactions did not make sense. You might find that you have overreacted to situations that trigger your anger. You will then be able to identify and understand how you can intervene to stop *reacting* and start *responding* differently to situations that anger you. The anger logs will become a map on how to manage your anger and prevent destructive outbursts.

How To Fill Out The Log

The log sheet has three columns and 17 rows. The first column tells you what you will write in the other two columns. The other two identical columns are for you to write in data for two separate events or situations that triggered your anger.

The first row is for you to write down the day, date, and the triggering situation when you became angry, for example, Saturday, April 17. The day and the date will tell you whether you have certain patterns like getting angry every Monday when you return to work.

The second row is for you write down the *thoughts* you had when you began getting angry, for example, "I'm not going to take his crap any more" or "She's always getting on my case."

In the third row write down the *physical feelings* you experienced in your body with your anger, for example, stomach knotting, face flushing, muscle tension, clenched fists.

The fourth row is for you to write down the *emotional feelings* you experienced as you became angry, such as frustration, rejection, put down, threatened, fear, anxiety, unsafe, attacked, etc.

Figure 4A
Sample of an Anger Log Sheet
(NO INTERVENTIONS USED)

	Monday 4/19	Tues 4/20
1. DAY AND DATE OF TRIGGERING EVENT	Monday 4/19 Argue about my work with boss.	Tues 4/20 Fight with wife — she was late without telling me.
2. WHAT I THOUGHT	He is a jerk!	Women use men and can't be trusted
3. MY PHYSICAL SENSATIONS	Headache, stomach in knot.	Knot in stomach, flushed face.
4. MY EMOTIONAL FEELINGS	Frustration, put down.	Rage, frustration, betrayed, lack of trust
5. INTENSITY OF MY ANGER	1 2 3 4 5 6 (7) 8 9 10	Yelled at her and left the house 1 2 3 4 5 6 7 8 (9) 10
6. MY BEHAVIOR AND ACTIONS	Argue back with him and begin to yell.	My wife and women in general
7. THE PERSON/THING MY ANGER FOCUSED ON	My boss for putting me down.	I'm not gonna take her crap
8. SELF-STATEMENTS I MADE	I can never do anything right.	None
9. ANGER ACTION OR RESPONSE TO SITUATION	None	None
10. SELF-RATING MY ANGER CONTROL	1 (2) 3 4 5 6 7 8 9 10	No time out 1 (2) 3 4 5 6 7 8 9 10
11. TAKE A TIME OUT? WHAT ELSE I DID	I didn't take a time out. I looked at a Playboy magazine.	Yes, till I got home
12. STUFF ANGER? HOW MUCH?	Yes, till I got home 1 2 3 4 5 6 7 (8) 9 10	1 2 3 4 5 6 (7) 8 9 10
13. INTENSIFY MY ANGER? HOW MUCH?	No 1 2 3 4 5 6 7 8 (9) 10	Thought about all the times I've been used by women who set me up 1 2 3 4 5 6 7 8 9 (10)
14. OTHER EMOTIONS?	Feeling stupid, not good enough	Feeling rejected
15. SUBSTANCE ABUSE?	Yes, had a beer after work	Drank beer, smoked pot
16. PHYSICAL ACTIVITY	None	None
17. POSITIVE SELF-TALK?	None	None

KEY: 1 = A little   10 = A lot

Learning to Track and Manage My Anger

Figure 4B
Sample of an Anger Log Sheet

(INTERVENTIONS USED)

1. DAY AND DATE OF TRIGGERING EVENT	Monday 4/19 Argue with Jeff on the job	Tues 4/20 Argue with wife — about money
2. WHAT I THOUGHT	He's being a royal jerk today! I wonder what his problem is?	We never have enough money to save anything! She's spending it all!
3. MY PHYSICAL SENSATIONS	Tension in my back and stiff neck	A headache
4. MY EMOTIONAL FEELINGS	Frustration	Frustration, worry
5. INTENSITY OF MY ANGER	1 2 3 4 5 ⑥ 7 8 9 10	1 2 3 4 5 6 7 8 ⑨ 10
6. MY BEHAVIOR AND ACTIONS	Suggest we talk after work	Suggest we read up on budgeting money
7. THE PERSON/THING MY ANGER FOCUSED ON	Jeff making it hard to work with him	Her spending money on clothes
8. SELF-STATEMENTS I MADE	I can work through this calmly	I care about her — I need to work out a plan to save money
9. ANGER ACTION OR RESPONSE TO SITUATION	Sit down with Jeff after work	Purchase a book on budgeting
10. SELF-RATING MY ANGER CONTROL	1 2 3 4 5 6 7 8 ⑨ 10	1 2 3 4 5 6 7 8 9 ⑩
11. TAKE A TIME OUT? WHAT ELSE I DID	Yes, took a 15-minute break	Yes, took an hour
12. STUFF ANGER? HOW MUCH?	No 1 ② 3 4 5 6 7 8 9 10	No 1 ② 3 4 5 6 7 8 9 10
13. INTENSIFY MY ANGER? HOW MUCH?	No 1 ② 3 4 5 6 7 8 9 10	No ① 2 3 4 5 6 7 8 9 10
14. OTHER EMOTIONS?	Insecure about working with Jeff	Scared about money and the new baby
15. SUBSTANCE ABUSE?	No	No
16. PHYSICAL ACTIVITY	Short walk	Jogged with Bill
17. POSITIVE SELF-TALK?	I know talking with Jeff will help	I can handle this situation

KEY: 1 = A little   10 = A lot

In row five you circle a number for the intensity of your anger at the time it happened. If you felt no anger you would circle 1, if you felt just a little anger you would circle 2 or 3. If you felt really angry you might circle 7 or 8. If you felt enraged, violent, and dangerous you would circle 10.

The sixth row is for you to write down what you did when you became angry. Did you hit someone? Throw or break things? Call someone names? Or did you try to calm yourself down? Relax and take deep breaths? Walk away from the situation?

The seventh row is for you to write down the focus of your anger. Were you angry at someone, your boss, womanfriend, parent, child, co-worker? Or was the focus of your anger on an object: flat tire, car, something you can't fix, your work?

In row eight you write down the statements you tell yourself (called self-talk), either negative statements (such as "I can't do this"; "I'm stupid"; "I can never do these things"; or "I'm not as good as he is"), or positive statements (such as "I can try this a different way"; "I'll get better at this if I keep practicing."; "I'll come back to this later").

The ninth row is for you to write down the anger action you took in this situation. Since you are working on trying to control your anger, we hope that you have done something productive with it. However, we recognize that you may have acted out your anger violently or acted in your anger toward yourself instead of controlling your anger. You will write down information here such as: "Told her I would take a time out and come back and talk with her about the problem." "Went down to the electric company with my canceled check to prove to them that I have paid the bill." "Asked my boss to have a meeting so I can explain my frustration with the guy I work with to her." "Went out jogging to get rid of some energy." Or, if you weren't able to control your anger, you might write, "Smashed my fist through the wall." "Went out drinking and crashed the car into a bridge abutment."

Learning to Track and Manage My Anger

The tenth row is for you to rate yourself on how well you think you controlled your anger. If you didn't control your anger at all and acted out or had an anger outburst you would circle 1. If you were able to control your anger somewhat by not acting out or hitting someone you would circle 2 or 3. If you were able to control your anger quite a bit and not get too upset, you would circle 5 or 6. If you were able to control your anger and not have any outbursts you would circle 8 or 9. If you took anger action to resolve the problem you would circle 10.

The next seven rows (11-17) are for you to note the actions you took when you realized you were getting angry.

The eleventh row is for you to write down whether you took a time out (described on page 66). If you did, list how long the time out was and what you did during the time out.

The twelfth row is for you to write down whether you stuffed your anger rather than doing something constructive to resolve the problem.

In the thirteenth row you write down whether you allowed your anger to intensify or escalate. Did you continue to push the issue that was triggering your anger and feed into the anger, allowing it to build?

The fourteenth row is where you can log other emotions you felt besides anger. Sometimes anger covers up unpleasant feelings you would rather not deal with, so you get angry instead.

The fifteenth row is for you to write down whether or not you used any drugs or alcohol to cope with the anger, calm you down, or ease the pain or frustration. Remember, drugs and alcohol do not solve your problems or make them go away. All they do is temporarily change your physical and mental feeling (sometimes for the better and sometimes for the worse) for a brief period of time. When you come down, the problem is still there, and it may be worse!

In the sixteenth row you write down what physical activity you may have done to spend some of your energy. Remember, anger is energy. When you take a time out one of the best things you can do during the time out period is a physical activity such as jogging, walking, shooting baskets, or playing another sport.

The seventeenth row is for you to write down any positive self-talk you do as a result of taking charge of your life and learning to control your anger. Self-talk is what you tell yourself about what is happening around you and what you think about the world. Examples of positive self-talk statements include: "I'm not going to let him push my buttons, it's not worth it"; "I can solve this problem if I put my mind to it"; "I've learned new skills and I don't have to let this get the best of me"; "I'm in control of my life."

A Place To Begin

If you have a short fuse or become angry very quickly, it is helpful for you to practice taking "time outs" or escaping the situation when you begin to sense your anger rising. Escaping the situation that is making you angry or taking a "time out" will help you slow down the anger process so that you will have time to think. If you have a short fuse, your anger may rise so quickly that you do not experience separate "risk factors" or "lapses" that give you a chance to use positive coping responses. If you have a short fuse, somebody calling you names, pushing you, picking a fight with you, and/or hitting you can trigger your anger and you go off in seconds.

Taking a time out is the way many people can temporarily escape the situation that they are getting angry about. Taking a time out does not mean that you are weak, backing down, or giving in. Taking a time out is taking control of your life. When you are in control of your life, others cannot control you.

Taking a time out means that for a limited period of time, you leave the situation that is feeding your anger. During the time out you take a break and let some energy out without using drugs or alcohol, or driving around in your car. You return after a pre-set time and try again to work out the problem. Preferably, when you take a time out you should take an hour. In some situations, such as at work, you may not be able to take an hour, but take as much time as you can without creating other difficulties. Remember to tell the other person that you will return and try to resolve the problem. If you don't come back and work on the problem, your time out will turn into a way of stuffing your anger.

Here's What You Do . . .

The next time you feel yourself getting angry, stop everything. Tell yourself that you do not need to get yourself worked up over any situation. If you are by yourself, just stop what you are doing. Change the activity that is getting you angry. If you are angry with another person, stop. Tell the person you are starting to feel angry and that you are going to take a time out. Then leave.

Make sure you use "I" statements such as, "I'm feeling angry and I want to take a time out." Remember *not* to blame the other person by saying things like, "You're making me angry" or "You're getting me pissed off." When you blame others for your angry feeling, you intensify the situation and escalate your anger.

If you find yourself getting angry with the same person over and over, wife, co-worker, friend, etc., advise the person that you are going to take time outs when you need them and that you will use the "T" sign to stop the conversation so you can take the time out. The "T" sign is the universal sign used by referees and others to signal a time out.

Once you have left the situation or person, make every attempt to take the time out for *one hour*. During that hour **DO NOT** think about the situation or event that angered you. While you are gone, do something physical to spend some energy, like walking or jogging. During this time do not talk to others about your problem.

Get the situation off your mind. Remember, **DO NOT** drink alcohol, use drugs, or drive around in your car.

When you return, if the situation involved another person, check in with the person and ask if the person is ready to begin discussing the problem again. If not, do not push the issue. Ask the person to set a time when the two of you can try again to resolve the problem.

Before you begin to talk about the problem, establish rules about how each of you will behave: 1) agree to use the "T" sign and take time outs; 2) agree not to call each other names; 3) agree to let the other person finish what he or she is saying; 4) agree to ask questions and clarify any issues you do not understand. Most important, acknowledge you both want to resolve the problem.

Just like a good slam dunk or three point basketball shot takes a lot of practice, so does the skill of using time outs to deal with your anger. If you don't practice taking time outs and using other interventions you learn in this workbook, you will not be very good at using them. Practice taking time outs. Your parked car is a good place to do this. When you are sitting in your car in the driveway or in the parking lot, pretend something has triggered your anger and practice taking your mind off of it by listening to music or sitting in the quiet. Try taking deep, slow breaths, about 10 of them. Practice this over and over again for ten minutes at a time. When you think you've got it down, keep on practicing. If you get into a traffic jam or hear something on the radio that angers you, practice taking a time out and relaxing.

One of the best ways to help you keep your commitment to yourself to use these techniques is to make a **Time Out Reminder Card**. You can write your personal time out contract on a 3" x 5" card and carry it with you in your pocket or in your wallet, so you'll have it wherever you go. Situations and your reactions change, so you should review and/or update your reminder card every month. Your reminder card should have the following sections on it:

REMINDER CARD SIDE 1

When I feel angry I will take a time out for one hour. If I am angry at another person, I will give the person the T sign to let him or her know I am calling a time out. I will tell the person that I am feeling angry and want to take a time out. I will advise the person that I will come back in one hour and ask if the person is willing to talk about the problem at that time.

During the time out I will do some physical activity such as jogging, walking, or playing sports. I will not think about the situation I got angry about. I will not use any alcohol or drugs.

REMINDER CARD SIDE 2

When I return from the time out I will check in with the other person and start by asking if we are both ready and willing to talk. If so, I will start by saying "I realize that part of the problem we are having is my fault."

While talking with the person I will try to resolve the problem by taking responsibility for my actions, not blaming others, owning my feelings and sharing them, and listening to the other person's point of view.

Chapter Four Exercises

EXERCISE #4-1: Anger Outburst/React vs. Anger Action/Respond

Make 3 columns in your notebook and label them "Situation," "Outburst/React," and "Action/Respond." In the first column, list 5 situations from your past or from your anger log where you got angry. In column 2, write down how you would behave in that situation with an anger outburst/reaction. In column 3 write down how you could behave differently with an anger action/response. Discuss this assignment with your counselor or a friend.

EXERCISE #4-2: Anger Log

Make five copies of the anger log sheet in Appendix A. Think about the last few times you were angry. Practice filling out the anger log sheets from those experiences. If you don't remember all of the details, fill each section out as you think it may have happened.

EXERCISE #4-3: Reminder Card

Get a 3" X 5" index card and make a time out reminder card. Review what you have written on the card with your counselor, group leader, or a friend. Carry it around with you from now on, and revise it when you notice your patterns or needs are changing.

EXERCISE #4-4: Time Out

Review the rules for taking a time out and practice taking short time outs at least twice a day.

Defense Mechanisms

What Are Defense Mechanisms?

Defense mechanisms are psychological tools people use in order to avoid dealing with thoughts or feelings that cause them pain. People use defense mechanisms to avoid guilt, blame, jealousy, grief, loss, and anger, among other feelings. Defense mechanisms are a form of self-protection that, like anger, can sometimes be helpful, but are self-destructively harmful most of the time.

Defense mechanisms can also block your getting anything out of your anger management program. People who become defensive are unable to recognize 1) that they have problems, and 2) how seriously those problems affect their lives. The more they use defense mechanisms, the harder it is for them to accept that they need help. Changing their thoughts, feelings, and behaviors to control their anger means looking deep within themselves at things that may cause them some emotional pain. When they don't recognize or accept their need to be in treatment, their involvement in an anger management program will be just on the surface, even when they think they really want to change. Their participation becomes an act, and those who get hurt the most in this well-meaning fraud are themselves. The lack of a deep personal commitment to change usually leads to falling behind in homework, failing to understand the problem, fears of being inadequate, and mistrust of almost everyone. If any of this rings a bell with you, it's a sign that you need to stop right now and take a look at yourself. Go back in your notebook and look at your answers to Assignment #2-1. Who have you hurt with your anger? Do you really want to keep doing that?

When you become defensive, sometimes you are unable to realize that you are using your defense tactics. You actually start to fool yourself. Sometimes you become so defensive that you need expert outside help to recognize and understand what your defense mechanisms are doing and which ones you are using. Eventually, you may have to stop and have someone point out to you the reasons why you are using your defense mechanisms to protect your pattern of anger. This is the case with George.

George has been angry for as long as he can remember. His anger grew and grew until he acted out violently at the age of 16 and was arrested for beating up his girlfriend and raping her. George blamed his girlfriend: "She shouldn't have called me a wimp! I had to show her I'm a man, and I don't take disrespect like that from anyone!" He never got into treatment for his anger problem or sex offending problem. At the age of 19 he had beaten and raped another girlfriend. Again, he blamed her for what he did to her. "She provoked me," he claimed, "She said I wasn't a real man."

By the age of 23, George was sitting in prison with a 3-year sentence for assaulting and raping his wife. At first he blamed her for "disobeying me." He blamed his victims, saying they were the ones with the problem and that he was the one who was the victim of their disrespect. George finally let his defenses down while in treatment.

In one exercise in his treatment program, George wrote down all the people on whom he had acted out his anger. In the second column he wrote the gender of each person he had named. In the third column, George wrote his relationship to the person. He was shocked to see that almost all of the names were of women he had been in sexual relationships with. The lists helped George recognize that *he* was the one with the problem. He was surprised when he let down his defenses enough to realize how one-sided his thinking had been.

Once you have accepted that you have problems, understand that you need help, and begin to work through your defenses, you are much more likely to be able to make healthy changes. When you accept your problems and acknowledge that you need and want help, then you won't waste your time fighting change. When you are actively involved in treatment, you will be able to change old patterns of thinking and behavior.

People who want to work on their problems do what it takes to get involved in treatment and to resolve their problem. If their defenses are getting in the way, they ask for help from others to point out when they are being defensive. They take an active stance ("What can *I* do to make this situation better, or to change *my* thinking about this situation?"). For the first time, they realize they have choices, and that they can choose to change and manage their anger better if they really want to. They practice their new behaviors and the interventions they've learned as they develop strategies to change. You can do this too.

Recognizing Defense Mechanisms

During treatment you have to deal with the guilt, shame, fear, and pain that you feel for yourself and for others. You may be using your defense mechanisms to avoid these feelings. However, in order to manage your anger better, you have to come to terms with these feelings. The first step is to recognize that you are using defense mechanisms. Listed below are six types of defense mechanisms. Do you recognize any of them in yourself?

1. RATIONALIZING. Rationalizing is making excuses and justifying your behavior, even though you know that what you are doing is wrong. Examples: "I wasn't doing anything wrong. I was just teaching her about sex. I have a right to get angry when I'm under a lot of stress."

2. INTELLECTUALIZING. When you intellectualize, you avoid dealing with the inner truth about your feelings. You make theories, but they don't make any deep connection to you or your behavior. You may say some of the right words about anger, or about offending behaviors, but it is always about *other people's* anger. In an attempt to avoid personal responsibility and change, you might say, "Oh, yes, I understand. The majority of expressed anger causes fear in the recipient." If you were *not* intellectualizing, if you were being honest about your feelings, you might say, "Oh, I understand. When I scream and yell at my wife and shove her against the wall, I'm terrorizing her. I'm bigger and stronger than she is and it isn't fair. But when I'm angry, I *want* her to be scared because that's the only way

Defense Mechanisms

she'll do it my way and stop contradicting me. When she contradicts me, I feel disrespected as a man." When you are intellectualizing, you hide your feelings behind generalizations or "research" (things you may have read that, taken out of context, tend to support your denial). An example: "Research shows that it is healthy to express anger as soon as it is felt." Someone may have written that, but the author was talking about the nonabusive expression of anger, not breaking furniture or threatening people.

3. DENIAL. When you deny, you refuse to admit the truth about your problems even though you know that it's true. You simply lie to yourself and others. You don't want to admit to yourself or others that you really did what you did, so you pretend that it didn't happen or that you weren't involved. There are different kinds of denial:

Responsibility. Denying responsibility is saying that you had nothing to do with the fight, the injury, the property damage, or any crime for which you may have been convicted. You deny any wrongdoing. Examples: "I didn't rape her. It wasn't me who broke the window. I didn't start the fight. I don't know what you're talking about."

Intent. Denying intent is admitting to doing the offensive behavior but denying that you did it on purpose. You are saying that you did not *intend* to do the offense, that it just "happened," or that it was an accident, so therefore it is not your fault and you are not responsible. Examples: "I didn't mean to do it. I don't know how it happened. All I did was duck—it's not my fault the bottle missed me and went through the window."

Harm. Denying harm is claiming that what you did to the victim of your anger caused no "real" harm. Most men with anger problems deny they've caused harm because no arms or legs were broken, no bodily harm is visible. They ignore that sexual, verbal, and physical assaults cause mental and emotional harm that is sometimes more damaging than bruises or broken bones. They can't connect with how the other person might have felt. They don't have empathy. Examples of statements denying harm: "He didn't get hurt. The beer bottle I threw hit the wall, not the kid. She's faking to get sympathy. I only punched the bed next to her head."

Frequency. Denying frequency is saying that the assaults didn't happen as often as the victim reports they occurred. Examples: "I only hit her once. I've only got into a couple of fights."

Intrusiveness. Denying the level of intrusiveness is stating that what you did was not as disturbing, invasive, or hurtful as the victim reports that it was. Examples: "Her blouse tore a little—I didn't rip it off. I pushed the door open—I didn't break it down."

Premeditation. This form of denial is claiming that you did not plan your crime or assault. It is denying that any thought went into what you did before you did it. Examples: "It just happened. I didn't plan it."

Minimization. When you minimize your behavior, you try to make it seem less serious than it really is. You downplay and under-state the truth about a situation. For example, you might claim "I only took her for a ride," when discussing a kidnapping, or "We just had sex," when talking about rape. Examples: "I only called her names—I didn't hit her. He's making a mountain out of a mole hill."

4. RELIGIOSITY. Many men with anger problems "see the light" and become super-religious after they seriously hurt someone they care about or after they are arrested for a violent episode. Practicing a religion can be a positive influence. We encourage you to develop the spiritual side of yourself. True spirituality supports your being responsible in your life. *Religiosity*, however, is different from spir-ituality and positive religious practice. It is often used as a defense mechanism, a way of using religion to *avoid* being responsible. Some people with anger problems make their religion an excuse not to involve themselves in treatment. They say, for example, "I don't need treatment, I've been forgiven." Elton, who had been arrested for several assaults, at one time said, "I do not need treatment because God has forgiven me and is healing me of my anger." He was hiding from his need to take responsibility for changing himself by using religiosity.

On the other hand, your sincere involvement in a religious practice can help you come to terms with your problems and may even help you make positive changes. But it cannot and should not be used as an excuse to avoid dealing with your past or present problems. Religion is not a shield to fend off dealing with real-life issues.

One last word on spirituality. One of the important tasks in maintaining a healthy lifestyle is to keep your life balanced. Imagine your life as a circle with five equal segments like a pie (see Figure 5). The pieces of your life are your Spiritual Self, Physical Self, Social Self, Thinking Self, and Feeling Self.

Each part of your self should be equal to every other part in order to for you to lead a healthy, balanced life. If any one part gets too large, your life becomes out of balance, like a wheel with a bulge in it. If you focus too much on religion, that part of your self gets larger and other parts of your self get smaller. Religion becomes an end in itself rather than a way to express your spirituality, and it turns into religiosity. When you ignore one part of your self to work on another there is usually a negative impact in the long run.

5. JUSTIFICATION. When you justify your behavior you make excuses for it, defend it, or explain it away. You do not take responsibility for what you do. For example: "I can't control my anger—it's hereditary, my father is the same way."

6. BLAME. People with anger problems often blame others for their anger. It is a way to not be responsible for what you do. For example, you hit someone and then blame the other person by saying, "He was looking for trouble."

Men with anger problems usually have a hard time with three issues: taking full responsibility for any violent or criminal behavior, letting go of their defense mechanisms, and managing their anger. Angry people have problems with their defense mechanisms getting in the way of dealing positively with their anger. Very angry people

Figure 5
Elements Of A Balanced Life

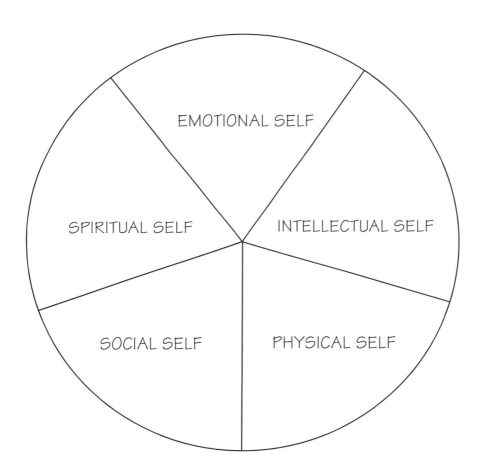

THE WHOLE SELF

The whole self consists of five separate parts. To keep your life healthy and well balanced you need to put about the same amount of time and energy into developing and maintaining each of these parts.

Defense Mechanisms

use their defense mechanisms so much that they don't even realize that they have them.

Your defense mechanisms are barriers you use to block yourself from being really involved in your anger management program. The good news is you can learn to overcome them. Your defensiveness does not have to be a big hurdle to making positive changes in your life. If you can say out loud to your treatment group, counselor, or friends that you use defense mechanisms and notice which defense mechanisms you use, you've made a big step toward managing your anger in nonhurtful ways. Once you can let down your defenses and keep an open mind about making changes in your life, then you can deal with the real issues of why you act out your anger violently.

Chapter Five Exercises

EXERCISE #5-1: Identifying My Defense Mechanisms

In your notebook or journal write down which defense mechanisms you are most likely to use.

EXERCISE #5-2: How I've Used My Defense Mechanisms

For each defense mechanism, describe two specific situations when you've used it.

Learned Anger Patterns

An important part of learning to manage your anger is understanding some of the ways you learned to express it. As we mentioned in Chapter Two, you learned many of your patterns of anger from the emotional environment of your childhood. Before you can break destructive cycles of abuse it is important to understand some of the emotions, thoughts, and events that influence your anger. These are called *precursors*. What you do with your anger today is likely to be a result of learning unhealthy patterns when you were younger.

Most people learn how to express their anger from family members. For example, if you were raised in a family where problems were openly and calmly discussed, you learned to talk about what bothers you. If your anger was met with a caring person talking with you and explaining why something happened, you learned that problems could be worked out and that yelling, hitting, shouting, threatening, and similar violent behaviors were unnecessary and wrong (of course, violent anger would then have had some shock value, and you could have learned to get what you wanted that way).

If you were raised in an environment where people yelled at each other and called each other names when they were angry, you learned to yell when you get angry. If you watched your parents and others hitting family members and perhaps other people, you learned that hitting is a way of expressing your anger. Other experiences, however, can also influence how you express your feelings and anger.

If you were hit when you did something wrong as a child, you probably cried the first few times. If you were told, "shut up before I *really* give you something to cry about," you learned to hide or stuff your feelings. If you were abused, you may have learned to cut yourself off from your feelings (keep them in or stuff them) in order to cope with the abuse. Hiding, stuffing, or cutting yourself off from your feelings was a means of surviving the abuse you experienced as a child living in an unhealthy environment. These survival tactics you practiced as a child soon became patterns of behavior that follow you into adulthood. This is what happened with Harry.

Harry's foster mother would punish him for the slightest thing he did wrong: for letting the screen door slam, for spilling a glass of water at the table, for scuffing up his school shoes, for forgetting to make his bed, and so on. Usually, she hit him hard across the hands, arms, legs, and buttocks with a wooden spoon. When Harry was little and he cried when she hit him, she told him, "Shut up or I'll *really* give you something to cry about!" Harry learned to keep the hurt, pain, and anger inside as a means of avoiding a worse beating. For Harry, keeping everything in meant survival.

When Harry grew up and left home, he continued to hide his feelings to protect himself from hurt. He never cried, even when his sister was killed in a car accident. He never showed any angry feelings, even when his workmate blamed him for a production screw-up. Finally, though, when Harry got fired without good cause, Harry blew up. He took a gas can down to the plant and started a fire. He spent 3 years in a forensic mental institution, then did 5-10 in prison.

When people develop unhealthy ways of coping or negative ways of expressing anger, they often get stuck there, using the same ways to deal with anger now that they used when they were kids. They haven't learned any new or better ways of expressing their anger. Even when the old unhealthy survival patterns work against you, you don't know what to replace them with—you haven't yet learned the new skills. People must be taught how to cope with situations that provoke anger and how to express anger in healthy ways. Fortunately you can be taught how to express your anger in healthy, assertive ways at any age. You're never too old to learn healthy behaviors. It just takes desire, motivation, and effort on your part.

The exercises at the end of this chapter are designed to 1) help you look at your childhood and how you were raised; 2) determine the precursors to your anger; and 3) pull together the components of your anger cycle. By doing the homework you will be able to work on changing your old, destructive anger patterns into healthier ways of dealing with anger.

The questions are based on how it was to grow up in your family and how your parents and siblings (brothers and sisters) related to each other, expressed their anger, and coped with angry situations. If you were raised by people other than your parents (other family members, relatives, in a foster home or institution, etc.) answer all of the questions with regard to your personal growing up experience. The exercises in this chapter may take you a long time to do. They are the basis for all the rest of your work on managing your anger, so take your time and make sure to answer them as completely and thoroughly as possible.

Chapter Six Exercises

EXERCISE #6-1: My Family

In your notebook, write down what you remember about the people who brought you up (your parents, step-parents, orphanage staff, etc). Were they usually angry, friendly, impatient, kind, rude, emotional, alcoholic, violent, etc.?

EXERCISE #6-2: My Family's General Behavior

What do you remember about what it was like in the family you grew up in? Was there a lot of laughter, crying, arguing, etc.? Did your family do things together, take vacations that were fun, go camping and fishing, etc.?

EXERCISE #6-3: Discipline

When you were a child and saw that somebody did something wrong, how was the person disciplined? How were you disciplined? Were you scolded, sent to your room, grounded, denied meals, spanked, struck with a hand, belt, or stick, etc.? Was violence used? How much or how often? *[Remember: violence you might have experienced never excuses violence you do.]*

EXERCISE #6-4: Abuse

In your family, did people abuse each other? For example, did your dad shove, hit, or beat your mother? Did your parents call each other or children in the family names, such as stupid, fat, ugly, bastard, etc.? What effects did it have on you? What were your thoughts about yourself?

EXERCISE #6-5: Your Anger

Thinking back to when you were a child, what happened when you became angry? What did you do and how did the other family members react?

EXERCISE #6-6: How Angry?

Looking back, how much of a problem do you think you had with anger as a child? Describe situations and give examples.

EXERCISE #6-7: Results of Anger

Describe how your anger was likely to get you into trouble.

EXERCISE #6-8: Substance Abuse

a) Did anyone in your family have a problem with drinking or drugs? Please describe what the problem was. Did this family member drink or take drugs before acting in a violent manner? If yes, describe what would happen.

b) Have you had a problem with drinking or drugs? Please describe what the problem was and when it began. Did you drink or take drugs before acting in a violent manner? If yes, describe what would happen.

EXERCISE #6-9: Present Relationships

Are there any similarities between how you were treated as a child and how you treat others today?

When I Get Angry

Patterns of Behavior

All of us have patterns of behavior. Thoughts, feelings, and behaviors you repeat usually become habits. Brushing your teeth every morning is a healthy habit. Getting drunk every Friday night is an unhealthy habit. Over time a group of habits becomes a cycle. One habit connects to another habit, that connects to another habit, that connects to the first habit. If you are not familiar with cycles of behavior you may want to ask a counselor or teacher who deals with repeated behaviors explain them to you. Each of us has cycles of anger that are a part of our behavioral pattern. These cycles repeat in similar situations.

Behavior Chains and Cycles

Behavior does not just "happen." Behavior is made up of a series of events. This series of events consists of thoughts, feelings, and behaviors. Each thought, feeling, and behavior can trigger another thought, feeling, and behavior, which can trigger another thought, feeling, and behavior, and so on. This series of thoughts, feelings, and behaviors makes up a *behavior chain*. The thoughts, feelings, and behaviors are the *links* in the chain (see Figure 6 on page 74).

Behavior chains that you repeat over and over can become a habit or cycle of behavior. Let's look at one cycle of behaviors that almost everyone does, though everyone does it a little bit differently—your morning routine or cycle.

Figure 6
A Behavior Chain

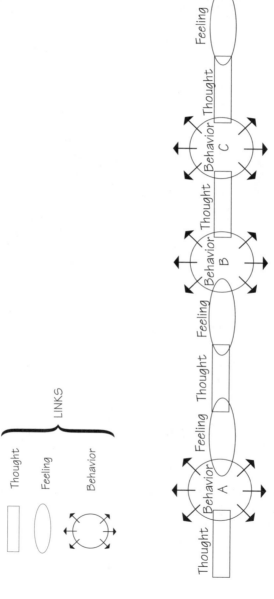

LINKS ARE CONNECTED
TO FORM A CHAIN

©1989, Laren Bays & Robert E. Freeman-Longo, *Why Did I Do It Again?*

A typical morning pattern or cycle is usually made up of several chains of behavior. The first chain is getting ready for work: shaving, showering, brushing teeth, and getting dressed. The next chain of behavior is preparing and eating breakfast. The next might be fixing lunch. Finally, the last chain is gathering everything—your lunch, jacket, car keys, papers, and whatever else you need—in one place before leaving for work. This morning cycle may follow certain thoughts, feelings, and behaviors that have become second nature, something you don't consciously notice. Cycles of behaviors are like old habits that you do without consciously thinking. We can stumble around, half awake/half asleep and get through most of these chains of behavior—if not all—because we are so familiar with them as a part of our daily routine.

Following your pattern of thoughts, feelings, and behaviors (*links*) in your morning cycle can help you better understand the chain of events in your other cycles of behavior. Look at just one part of a behavioral chain: making coffee in the morning. Fixing your coffee might happen in a chain like this: 1) you pour clean cold water into the coffee maker (*behavior*); 2) you say to yourself, "I'll make 6 cups this morning," (*thought*) as you pour the water into the coffee maker; 3) you may begin to get excited (*feeling*) as you look forward to sipping on a fresh brewed cup of good hot coffee; 4) after the coffee is made, you *think* about adding cream and sugar and 5) you pour (*behavior*) both into your cup; 6) as you take the first sip you *feel* content and 7) *think* about taking a thermos of coffee to work; 8) you reach (*behavior*) for the thermos in the cupboard, and so on.

Isaac and his wife almost always argue over money. When they fall behind with their bills Isaac gets upset. When he thinks that his wife Betty has not spent money wisely, he blames their financial problems on her. When she points out that none of her purchases were unnecessary, Isaac gets more angry and throws the checkbook on the floor. He then goes down to the bar and spends money (money that he has just pointed out they don't have) on drinking beer. Isaac's pattern is to drink beer at the bar when he gets angry.

As you can see from this example, chains of thoughts, feelings and behaviors can follow one another and become *linked* together. When they are linked together and repeat themselves over and over again, they form cycles. For example, if you get angry when you have a disagreement with someone, the chances are that you deal with your anger in the same way each time. Look at Isaac's pattern in the story on the previous page.

You may find that you have similar cycles of behavior. You may isolate yourself from others and withdraw when you are angry or have arguments. Or, you may find that every time you get angry you end up yelling at other people, or become physical and hit people and/or break things.

Anger Patterns

People tend to have one way, or maybe a few particular ways, of reacting to situations that anger them. For example, at work you may get angry and react one way to being ignored when you ask someone a question, while you react in a totally different way when the same thing happens at home. Below are examples of anger patterns. Some of them may be similar to your cycle(s) of anger.

WITHDRAWAL/ISOLATION. Anger may result in withdrawing from others or isolating. In many cases there is no communication about your anger with others. Thus, when you are angry with someone, the other person may never know because you withdraw and/or isolate yourself.

Some people use their anger as an excuse to withdraw. In other words, they find something to get angry about as an excuse to work themselves up into a bad mood so others will stay away. Other people naturally avoid being around the angry person. As a result, the angry person is easily able to withdraw/isolate. By deliberately becoming angry, they set up the situation in order to keep others away.

YELLING/SHOUTING. Anger may result in yelling at others and having a shouting match. This behavior almost always puts the other person(s) on the defensive. The problem that caused the anger is seldom resolved and the anger continues. You may even end up calling the other person names.

THREATS. In some situations, individuals get angry and think they can solve their problems by threatening to harm other people or their property. Threats are especially powerful when made against people who are afraid of the angry person, and may be powerful with strangers. Threats can lead to physical fighting.

Some people like to fight when they get angry. When they get angry and want to fight they try to provoke others into fighting by making challenges or threatening the other person. When you feel bad about yourself, you may even pick a fight as a way of feeling more powerful than the other person, as a way of feeling better when the targeted person caves in to your threats.

SHOVING/SLAPPING/PUNCHING. Some people get angry and immediately lash out at others. They may shove, slap, or punch the person they are angry at to hurt the other person or make the person feel scared or bad. Often, this reaction is out of fear. By lashing out physically, the hope is to push the other person away, or to make the person do what you want. Shoving, slapping, and punching is the way some people try to have power and control over others. People who hit, slap, and/or punch often have low impulse control. In other words they have a short fuse.

VIOLENCE. In its extreme form, anger is expressed in violent acts. It is deliberate and forceful. Physical fighting is violence. Repeatedly hitting, punching, beating or trying to run someone over with a car is violence. Violence in its extreme form can and often does result in death.

Many people demonstrate a combination of these patterns. These patterns all begin with warning signs that you are becoming angry. These warning signs are a part of the anger cycle that each of us experiences; they include thoughts, feelings (both physical and emotional), and behaviors as we described earlier.

As you begin to explore your patterns of anger, pay special attention to the **cues**, or warning signs, that you are getting angry.

Try to identify the **thoughts** you have that feed your anger. Some of these thoughts include:

- *Who does she think she is?*
- *I'll teach him a lesson he'll never forget.*
- *No one's gonna push me around.*
- *You just wait!*

Coupled with these thoughts are **feelings** you experience that result from your anger building up. Some of these feelings are emotional and may include:

- Rage
- Resentment
- Powerless
- Frustration
- Rejection
- Losing control

You may experience **physical sensations** that may include:

- Muscle tension (tightness in your jaw, neck, arms or legs)
- Headache
- Stomach upset
- Sweaty palms
- Flushing of the head, neck, and face (turning red and warm)
- Increased heart rate
- Rapid breathing
- Narrowed vision

Finally, there are **behaviors** you engage in that support and or feed your anger, including:

- Alcohol and substance use/abuse
- Pacing
- Brooding, playing the situation that angers you over, and over, and over in your mind.

When your behavior chains link onto each other, they become a cycle. For example, look at Jake's behavior chains in the next story.

Cycles of Anger

In most cases, you have two basic options when you become angry. One option is to get caught up in your destructive anger cycle. We refer to this as the *react* or *anger act-out cycle*. In this cycle you tend to stuff your anger, escalate the situation that triggered your anger, and/or react to the anger and act out. Even though there may be some planning on your part, you tend to lash out in anger and then you may feel bad about it afterwards. The other option is the

response or anger/ action cycle. This is the healthy way of dealing with your anger. We will explain this cycle later.

To help you understand your anger, we have divided the anger cycle into four phases (see Figure 7) that are explained below.

Everyone's cycle is not the same. Your cycle may take hours for your anger to build up while another person's anger can build up in minutes. That means that your build-up phase would be the largest portion of your anger cycle while the next person's build-up phase is the smallest part of his cycle. So, don't compare yourself to others.

Even though the phases of the cycle come in order (**Pretends To Be Normal, Build-Up, Act Out,** and **Downward Spiral**), the parts of each phase may not. Once you experience the triggering event in one situation, your

On Friday, Jake thinks he is doing okay, although it has been a hard week. He got yelled at for being late to work Monday. Tuesday he sneaked out of work early because he was depressed and wanted to stop for a drink on the way home. Wednesday he and Melissa got into a fight so loud that a neighbor called the cops, but he talked his way out of that one. Thursday he was late again.

Now it's Friday, nothing bad has happened, and Jake can't wait to cash his paycheck and get to the Bull and Stein, his favorite bar. He'll drink a lot with people he calls his friends. He'll play some pool with someone new—not a regular—who will accuse him of cheating (since he really does cheat). Jake will threaten the newcomer, and start a fight. Chances are that Jake will win—he's done this many times before—and then he'll have to pay the bar owner for the stuff that got broken.

Saturday and Sunday, he does his drinking at home in front of a football game. Sunday night he'll want to go down to the Bull and Stein again, but he's broke, so he'll start an argument with Melissa, saying that she spends too much money on her clothes. He'll get mad, take money out of her purse, and stomp off down to the bar, where he'll drink until his money runs out.

Monday he'll be late to work again because he's hungover and stiff from the fight he got into on Friday night, and the whole series of behavior chains will begin again. Jake's anger cycle is running his life.

next link could be **feelings** of anger, while in another situation, the next link could be a **thought** that leads to other **feelings**, such as embarrassment.

When I Get Angry

Figure 7
Chains Become An
Anger Act-Out Cycle

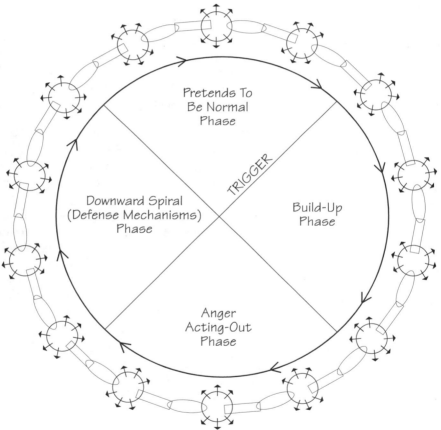

Thought

Feeling

Behavior

} LINKS
IN THE
CHAIN

Pretends To
Be Normal
Phase

TRIGGER

Downward Spiral
(Defense Mechanisms)
Phase

Build-Up
Phase

Anger
Acting-Out
Phase

© 1994 Murray Cullen & Robert E. Freeman-Longo. Adapted with permission from *Why Did I Do It Again*, © 1989 Laren Bays & Robert E. Freeman-Longo.

The phases of the anger cycle shown in Figure 7 are explained below. As a reminder, the links in the chain that feed your anger consist of *thoughts, feelings*, and *behaviors*. This explanation of the anger cycle contains more details than we can easily show in Figure 7. You will need this extra information in order to fill out your own anger cycle later on.

PRETENDS TO BE NORMAL PHASE

In this phase of your anger cycle, everything appears to be going smoothly. We call this "Pretends To Be Normal" because in reality, your life is not normal. The anger problem you have still exists and is in some way running your life. In the Pretends To Be Normal phase, the anger is not actively a problem but it lies just below the surface. You can get into your anger cycle and explode with a triggering event even when your life appears to be running smoothly and there are no obvious or important problems.

Trigger. The *trigger* is the event or situation that sets off your anger cycle. Often you are triggered when someone says or does something that bothers you. In a split second your mind races to past events and "old tapes" (also called self-talk) that lead to your anger. You may focus on these past negative events or situations. Triggers are high-risk factors for anger outbursts.

BUILD-UP PHASE

The *Build-Up Phase* is the part of your cycle where you allow your anger to build. You may even feed your anger in order to help it build quicker. During this phase you have the opportunity to *intervene* in your anger and work at changing it to be positive anger. Positive anger will help you take action against the problem. Negative anger will contribute to further problems and keep you locked into your hurtful anger cycle.

BUILD-UP PHASE (continued)

The Build-Up Phase is where your behavioral chains of *thoughts, feelings,* and *behaviors* may be easiest to see. Remember that there is no strict order for your thought, feeling, and behavior links. They may occur as behavior → feeling → thought, or thought → behavior → thought → feeling → feeling → behavior, or any combination. Also contributing to the Build-Up Phase are your physical sensations, the fight-or-flight reactions we discussed in Chapter Two. These sensations are also called *anger arousal.*

Thoughts. After an event triggers your anger cycle you begin to experience specific thoughts that are a part of your anger cycle. These thoughts (tapes) are old messages and ways of thinking you may have learned in childhood from family members or other adults who themselves have had anger problems. For example, these "old tapes" may be *thinking errors* such as "Women are all the same—they just use men," or "Nobody cares—people are out to screw me over," or "I can't trust anyone."

Feelings. Thoughts and behaviors are often linked to specific emotions such as fear, anxiety, anger, guilt, depression, frustration, shame, sadness, fury, rejection, insecurity, inadequacy, helplessness, hopelessness, rage, and so on.

Anger arousal is the body sensations that come with your anger. These body sensations or feelings are cues associated with anger—that is, they help you become aware that you are getting angry. For example: tension, stiffness, muscle aches, tightness, heart pounding or racing, rapid breathing, high blood pressure, feeling hot or flushed, upset stomach, and so on.

Behaviors can come before or after thoughts and feelings. When you are in your cycle, you generally

**BUILD-UP
PHASE
(continued)**

behave in certain ways (often out of habit) that set up situations so you can act out your anger, for example: using alcohol and other drugs, or hanging around others who will feed your anger. Three kinds of behaviors that contribute to the Build-Up Phase of your anger cycle are *addictive behaviors, fantasy*, and *planning*.

Addictive Behaviors. Many people who have anger problems also have problems with drugs. They drink a lot of alcohol and/or use other drugs to escape reality, to build up their courage, to cope with pain, or to avoid problems. Others use masturbation, overeating, or overworking to avoid problems and escape from unpleasant situations.

Fantasy. Many people who are angry get into a fantasy or a kind of daydream about what they will do, to others, to themselves, to other people's property, and so on. The fantasy is a way of planning or premeditating your anger act by seeing in your mind the way you want to act out.

Planning is setting up the anger act/anger outburst to occur. Examples might include: 1) going to specific places, such as bars or taverns; 2) certain behaviors, such as looking to buy drugs, drinking, mentally rehearsing how you are going to tell someone off or beat someone up, and so on. Many people with anger problems try to convince themselves and others that their anger outbursts "just happened." They describe their actions as "impulsive" (happening at the spur of the moment). This is a kind of denial or excuse-making—whatever you do to act out your anger is really *planned* impulsiveness. Anger doesn't "just happen." Before you hit or yell at somebody, you make a decision (even if it is a quick

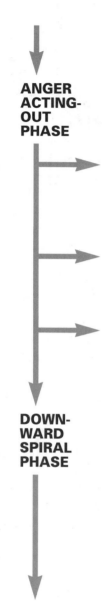

ANGER ACTING-OUT PHASE

DOWN-WARD SPIRAL PHASE

decision) to do it. When you take the time (however short) to think about making a decision, you are *not* being impulsive.

This is the anger act (outburst). The anger outburst is the release of built-up anger, expressed in a variety of ways: *verbal* abuse of others, *physical* abuse of others or destruction of property, or *self-abuse*.

Verbal. You express your anger verbally by calling others names, yelling, screaming, arguing, provoking people, making fun of how others look, making negative or sexually suggestive comments about their companions, etc.

Physical. Your anger is expressed through destroying property/objects, or injuring the person such as hitting, punching, biting, kicking, battering, sexual abuse, rape, incest, etc.

Self-abuse. Suicide attempts, alcohol/drug abuse, other self-abusive or self-destructive behaviors are ways you act your anger out towards yourself. Self-abuse is just as destructive as acting out your anger towards someone else.

After acting out your anger you may feel remorse for what you have done or feel bad about your actions. If you have destroyed property, hurt somebody, hurt yourself, etc., right afterwards you may feel sorry about (regret) what you did. After acting out, it is common to feel 1) guilt about what you have done, 2) shame about who you are, and 3) embarrassment over your actions (thinking of your anger as stupid, etc.). Often you start using your defense mechanisms, including justification, rationalization, denial, minimization, and so on.

DOWN-WARD SPIRAL PHASE (continued)

Next you may feel *false remorse*. With false remorse, you may try to cover your tracks (for example, if you hit your child and caused an injury, you tell the doctor the child fell down the stairs). Or, you try to make it up to the person you dumped your anger on (apologizing to your wife if you hit her, or buying her flowers or gifts). Another example of behavior resulting from false remorse is doing something "generically" good to compensate for your hurtful anger actions, and to avoid having to think of yourself as doing bad things to others. An example of "generic goodness": Greg screamed at and shoved his wife, and while out walking off his energy, he felt bad. When he saw a guy on crutches trying to get into the corner store, he rushed ahead to hold the door open. Greg gets to feel "good" about himself because he's the kind of thoughtful person who holds doors for strangers on crutches, and meanwhile he's excusing himself for how badly he has treated his wife.

PRETENDS TO BE NORMAL PHASE

Next you may experience a mood of *false resolve*. In this mode you tell yourself, "I will never do this again," or, "I will control my anger and not let it get out of hand again." The false resolve usually moves you back into the **Pretends To Be Normal Phase.**

The other option for expressing anger is the non-destructive release of your anger we call your *Anger Action Cycle*. This is a new way of viewing angry situations and learning how to manage your anger. There are still four major phases in the anger action cycle, but they are different from the phases of your Anger Act-Out Cycle (see Figure 8 on page 87).

The **Normal** phase is similar to the *Pretends* to Be Normal phase of your Anger Act-Out cycle. The difference is that you are not *pretending* that everything is okay. You acknowledge that you have an anger problem and use interventions to help you manage your anger in nonhurtful ways. Your *triggers* may or may not remain the same. That is, after working on your anger, you may find that events that used to trigger your anger no longer get you upset. You recognize the event or situation for what it is and you work it through instead of feeding your anger and escalating the risk situation. Other triggers may still get you upset and set off the feelings of anger, but you don't let your anger build up. Instead you start using relaxation, avoidance, and escape strategies along with other interventions and techniques as soon as you start feeling yourself get angry.

A part of learning to manage your anger is identifying thoughts, feelings, behaviors, and situations that may *trigger* it. You will want to review closely the thoughts, feelings, behaviors, and situations in your past that trigger and/or feed into your anger. Then you will want to work on avoiding identified triggers whenever possible and learning how to get out of situations that tend to trigger your anger.

In the **Normal Phase** you work at avoiding these *triggers* and situations that are likely to activate your anger. This may include choosing new friends, changing your behavior (for example, by not going to bars and taverns and drinking or not hanging out in places where people get into fights). If your job is a high risk factor for your anger, and if the parts of it that are most triggering can't be changed, you may need to change jobs.

In the **Build-Up Phase** you may find yourself getting angrier or remaining angry at a situation, but you are using the new coping responses you are learning to *limit* how angry you let yourself get and to *reduce* the intensity of your anger.

In the **Build-Up Phase** you still have *thoughts, feelings,* and *behaviors* that are connected to your anger. However, you are able to replace the old thoughts, feelings, and behaviors with new thoughts, feelings, and behaviors that help you decrease the extent of your anger while you work at trying to resolve the problem. You don't let yourself get so angry so quickly. You stop and think about what's

Figure 8
An Anger Action Cycle

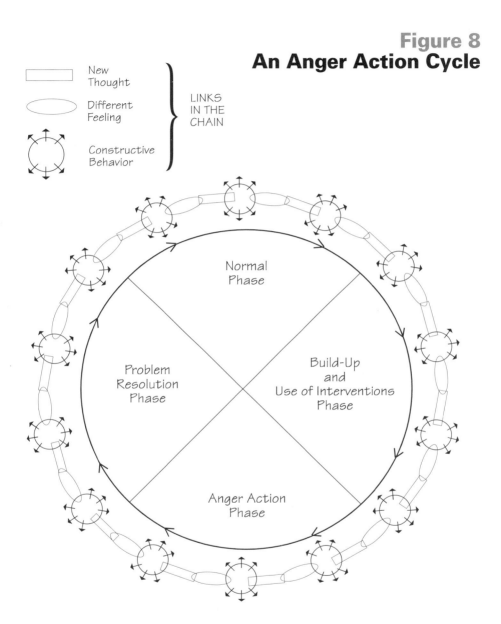

really going on instead of having a knee-jerk reaction to something somebody said. You remember your Situation Perception Training (you can review it in Chapter Four). You look at whose problem this situation really is, and whether what the other person said means something about you or something about the person who said it. Paul found a new way to deal with street insults.

Paul was walking in his neighborhood, when some guys on the corner yelled out, "Hey, I slept with your mother last night!" Paul used to get angry at this kind of taunting. But since he's been working on his anger, he reacts differently. First he took a couple of deep breaths. Then he thought, "I know this is not true. This guy must really be pathetic if the only way he can feel good about himself is to use sex to try to insult someone's mother." He just shrugged his shoulders and kept going.

Instead of *acting out* your anger in the third phase of the cycle, you take whatever steps are necessary in order for you to resolve the problem that you are feeling angry about. You take **Anger Action** to correct the problem. By taking appropriate action to correct the problem, you are expressing your anger in a constructive, nonhurtful way and trying to work towards fixing the problem. You replace the old ways of acting out with new ways of taking **action** to resolve your anger.

The last phase of the anger action cycle is the **Problem Resolution Phase**. *Resolution* is working on resolving the problem that generated your anger. *Resolution* is using skills, interventions, and problem solving techniques that help you manage your anger in the future. This takes time, effort, and practice.

In the **Problem Resolution Phase**, it is important that you take the time both to work on resolving the problem(s) that triggered your anger *and* to give yourself positive feedback for changing your old, destructive angry ways. When you work through a problem, use positive self-talk as a reminder that you can manage your anger in a way that moves you toward resolving problems rather than making them worse. Ask others for feedback on how you're doing. When others around you have seen the "old you" angry in the old way, they will begin to recognize that you're more approachable now that you are managing your anger. Don't be embarrassed or ashamed to ask for their opinion. Nobody likes being around angry people. Your friends and family can also tell you how well you are doing, since they will feel better when they aren't exposed to your angry outbursts.

NORMAL PHASE

In this phase of your **Anger Action Cycle,** things run more smoothly because you are working with your anger, and the problems that feed your anger, in order to improve your life. When you begin to manage your anger, your life becomes more *"Normal"* because anger is not the driving force behind how you feel and it is not running your life. Managing anger does not mean not feeling angry. You will still experience anger, but now you are managing it in a healthy, productive fashion. In the Normal phase, your life is going along well. There is no old, unresolved anger just below the surface ready to erupt when triggered. You may begin to feel angry, but you are less likely to explode, and more likely to take action to correct the problem that is generating the anger.

Trigger. You still experience *triggering* events or situations that result in your feeling angry. In the **Anger Action Cycle,** however, you are aware of your triggers and therefore more prepared to work on not letting anger get the best of you when someone says or does something that bothers you. You can use escape strategies when you are not able to avoid triggers. Instead of moving into escalating your anger and making the situation worse, you move into the **Build-Up and Use of Interventions Phase.**

**BUILD-UP
& USE OF
INTER-
VENTIONS
PHASE**

In your **Anger Action Cycle,** the *Build-Up Phase* is present because you will still experience feeling angry. Everyone experiences anger from time to time. The difference between this phase in your anger cycle and your anger action cycle is how you work with the different links in the chain. Instead of your mind racing to past events and "old tapes" and focusing on past negative events and situations, you use the tools and interventions you have practiced to avoid an anger outburst. As soon as you discover the triggering event, you work to resolve the problem or your feelings instead of escalating them. That may mean talking with a friend or a counselor who is not involved in the immediate situation in order to resolve feelings about a problem that you may not be able to change.

Thoughts. In this cycle, after an event triggers your anger, you self-correct your old tapes and replace them with positive self-statements and thoughts such as:

- I can handle this situation
- There are different solutions to the problem
- I don't need to lose it or get worked up
- What can I do to begin resolving the problem

Feelings. Even when you have learned to manage your anger, you will still experience a variety of painful emotions such as fear, anxiety, guilt, depression, frustration, shame, sadness, rejection, and so forth. Having these emotions is *normal.* In your **Anger Action Cycle,** you allow yourself to experience your feelings and take the time at some point during the day to reflect on them and talk them out with someone you care about and trust. Talking through your feelings helps you understand them. Feelings are normal.

**BUILD-UP
& USE OF
INTER-
VENTIONS
PHASE
(continued)**

**ANGER
ACTION
PHASE**

Anger arousal. You are likely to still experience the body sensations associated with your anger. Everyone experiences these body sensations when angry. Tension, muscle stiffness, heart pounding or racing, rapid breathing, high blood pressure, and a flushed face are common, normal feelings people experience when they are angry. But in your **Anger Action Cycle,** you remember that regardless of how intense these sensations feel, they will pass. You don't let these sensations stampede you into a fight-or-flight reaction. You are able to practice deep breathing and relaxation to help decrease your physical anger arousal and prevent an anger outburst. Remember, it is impossible to relax and be angry at the same time. Practice relaxation as often as you can.

Behaviors. Behaviors are still part of your response to your feelings of anger. The goal in your **Anger Action Cycle** is to behave in ways that will help you take action to *resolve* the problem, not escalate it. In your **Anger Action Cycle,** the goal is to **avoid** the three kinds of behaviors (*addictive behaviors, fantasy*, and *planning*) that contribute to acting out your anger destructively.

In the **Anger Action** phase, you take action to remedy the situation that has led to the anger. This may involve talking to people involved in the situation or doing something to correct the problem. Each situation can be different so it is important that you have as many resources and options available to you as possible in order to avoid escalating your anger and acting it out. The kind of action you take (instead of having an anger outburst) is very important in learning to manage your anger.

When I Get Angry

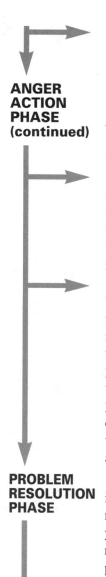

ANGER ACTION PHASE (continued)

Verbal. The anger action you take can be *verbal*, talking through the problem and trying to resolve your anger through appropriate discussion. You might try writing out what your view of the problem is to help you present it calmly later. Writing in a journal about a situation you cannot change may help you resolve your own feelings about it without resorting to a destructive angry outburst.

Physical. Instead of hitting, fighting, or physically abusing someone, you engage in a physical activity such as sports, jogging, walking, etc., to release your anger energy. After you work off your anger energy, then you come back to work on the problem later,

Self-care. Instead of being self abusive (such as by using alcohol and drugs), you engage in behavior that helps you take care of yourself and decrease any negative impact of your anger. Exercise, relaxation, time-outs, talking out the problem, doing something you enjoy, thinking about the problem and better ways to resolve it, writing in a journal, rewarding yourself for handling the situation constructively, even taking a hot shower or a sauna to relax are all ways you can better care for yourself instead of abusing yourself.

PROBLEM RESOLUTION PHASE

The last phase of your new **Anger Action Cycle** is the *Resolution* phase. In this phase you have either resolved the situation that generated your anger or you are actively working on the situation in order to resolve it. Perhaps you've tried to resolve the problem without success or the problem just cannot be resolved by your individual effort. You can use the **Resolution** phase to prevent yourself from getting into the same situation in the future or to

NORMAL PHASE

learn how to respond better (more effectively or with better self-care) the next time. Working on resolving the problem, you boost your self-esteem, avoid the "Downward Spiral" phase of your anger cycle, and move into the **Normal Phase**.

Why Study My Cycles of Behavior?

The reason for studying these cycles of behavior is they are the basis of how we act. Cycles directly and indirectly affect our lives and the lives of those around us. The following are reasons why it is important for you to understand your cycles of behavior:

• You learn what led up to your committing an aggressive or violent act or even a criminal offense. When they have been arrested for stabbing or beating up someone, many men ask themselves, "How did I get to the point of doing this?" They tell themselves, "I'm not that kind of person. How could I have done that?" The path from normal behavior to a criminal act is not hard to see once you look at things in perspective. By understanding your cycle and mapping out the distinct parts of it, you can identify, understand, and eventually change the decisions and behaviors that led to your aggression.

• You see how your actions have a cause and effect. Think back to the example of Lance who had coffee spilled on him. Lance could have reacted in several ways. His reaction depends on how he interprets the situation and who the person was that spilled coffee on him. With one interpretation involving a stranger, the event could have ended up in a verbal assault or a physical fight.

• You learn about your thoughts, your feelings, and your behaviors that cause you to behave the way you do around others. In addition, you begin to recognize that others have their own cycle(s) of anger. This recognition may give you some indication of how others think, feel, and act towards you. For example, if you are asking somebody about an important issue and you are clenching your fist, raising your voice, and showing other physical anger cues, that person may be intimidated by you or become angry with you (thinking you are confronting them) when you think you are making a simple inquiry.

Similarly, you will soon learn how to identify the parts of another person's anger cycle. In learning this skill, you may be able to help de-escalate the other person's anger before it sweeps you up and carries you into an aggressive or violent confrontation.

• You will become more aware of how you usually react to various thoughts, feelings, and environments. This is very important because you may tend to go to places where trouble is sure to occur. For example, if you are an alcoholic and you become violent when you drink, then going to bars, pool halls, or even to friends' houses to watch the World Series or the Super Bowl is not a good idea when you know they will serve alcohol. If you are somebody who gets into fights easily, then you need to avoid places where people get into fights, such as hockey games.

• Understanding and tracking your cycle will teach you that your behavior is affected by places you go, things you see, and sounds or words you hear. We have already explained the relationship between your thoughts, feelings, and behaviors in relation to the triggering situation or environment. Different situations, your friends, your work place, even the movies influence the way that you think, feel, and act.

• Understanding your cycle will teach you how your feelings influence your behavior.

• You will learn how your thoughts influence your behavior.

• You will learn how your beliefs about the world and yourself influence your behavior.

• Understanding your cycles teaches you that what you do today will have an effect on what you do tomorrow and in the future.

Increasing your awareness and understanding your anger cycle will teach you when and how to stop your aggressive behavior. It is important for you to realize what happens when you become angry. Please pay special attention to the assignments at the end of this chapter.

Chapter Seven Exercises

EXERCISE #7-1: Anger Situations

In your journal write down as honestly as possible what happens when you become angry. (By doing this, you can alert yourself in the future that you are becoming angry before the anger leads to aggression). For example, "Here are the typical *situations* that make me feel very angry and I usually wind up . . ."

EXERCISE #7-2: Emotions that Feed My Anger

Look back over the last several times that you became seriously angry and aggressive. In your notebook write down the *situations* and the *feelings* you remember experiencing during these times.

EXERCISE #7-3: Physical Anger Cues

When you think about the situations you described in Exercise #7-2, you can probably recall that your body gave you cues that you were becoming angry. For example, your heart might have started beating faster, your ears may turn red, your hands start feeling sweaty, the arteries in your neck pop out, etc. Write down the anger arousal signs or *cues* (physical sensations) that your body gives you that you are becoming angry.

EXERCISE #7-4: Anger Thoughts

Refer again to the situations you described in Exercise #7-2. Write down the *thoughts* that went through your mind when you became angry in these situations.

EXERCISE #7-5: Anger Behaviors

Refer to Exercise #7-2, and write down the things you did *(behaviors/actions)* when you become angry (such as yelling, punching, kicking, stabbing, drinking, overeating, etc.). Include verbal, physical, and self-abusive behaviors.

EXERCISE #7-6: Anger Patterns

Now refer back to the description of patterns of anger in this chapter. Write down patterns of anger that describe you when you become angry.

EXERCISE #7-7: Anger Act-Out Cycle

On a separate page in your notebook, draw a large circle. Divide the circle into four sections (remember the sections don't have to be the same size—if your Build-Up Phase is longer than your Acting Out Phase, make it bigger). Fill in the names of the anger act-out cycle phases. Taking one of your past anger outbursts, write in a short description of what triggered your anger. Write in your thoughts, feelings, and behaviors for each phase. If there's not enough room, write some of them outside the circle with a line pointing to the phase where they occurred. Explain your cycle to your group, counselor, or friend.

EXERCISE #7-8: Anger Action Cycle

On another page in your notebook, draw another circle and divide it into four sections. Fill in the names of the Anger Action Cycle phases. Taking the same outburst you diagrammed in Exercise #7-7, write in corrective thoughts, feelings, and behaviors that might have helped you respond differently to the triggering situation and avoid a destructive anger outburst. Include self-care actions. In the Anger Action phase, write in some actions you might have taken toward resolving the situation. In the **Resolution** phase, write in how the situation might have been resolved. Explain this cycle to your group, counselor or a friend.

EXERCISE #7-9: Two Cycles

Look at the two cycles you have diagrammed. Where are they similar or the same? Where do they begin to be different? Write about the differences, then explain them to a friend or your group.

Chapter Eight
Anger Management & Relapse Prevention

U p to this point you have learned about anger, cycles of behavior, and cycles of anger. You have looked at how your early experiences with anger affect how you express anger now. You should be keeping an anger log and begin to see patterns in the ways you act out your anger. You have begun to understand how thoughts, feelings, and behaviors in certain situations lead you into your anger cycle. You saw in the last chapter how to break down your Anger Acting Out cycle into its four phases. And you saw what a healthier Anger Action cycle might look like. All this learning, reading, and homework is providing you with a solid foundation for learning the actual techniques of anger management. Just as you can't build a house without a solid foundation, neither can you manage your anger successfully without a solid foundation.

The last piece of your foundation is called Relapse Prevention (RP). **RP** is defined as "a process for emotional (feelings), cognitive (thinking), and behavioral (actions) self-management of a problem behavior." It is the process of taking control of your life with help, support, and monitoring by your family, friends, co-workers, or (if you have committed a criminal offense) parole officer. Relapse Prevention was originally developed to help people with substance abuse problems and was later adapted to help people manage many other kinds of problems.[1]

---

[1] Many of the terms and ideas explained in this chapter are based on G. Alan Marlatt and J.R. Gordon's work *Relapse Prevention,* published by Guilford Press, New York, 1985.

RP can be used to help you manage your anger. If you have learned RP in another program, such as drug rehab, you can use the same concepts to help you manage your anger cycle in a way that doesn't hurt others or yourself. The relapse process happens in the first two parts of your anger cycle, the **Pretends To Be Normal** phase and the **Build-Up** phase. When you work on your Relapse Prevention skills, you are much less likely to get to the **Acting Out** phase. Instead, you'll get into your **Anger Action** and **Resolution** phases. Figure 9 outlines Relapse Prevention for managing your anger.

Let's look at the various components of RP as it can be applied to anger management.

Calm and In Control
(Abstinence From Acting Out Your Anger)

The goal of anger management is for you to avoid acting out your anger in the nonproductive and/or destructive ways you have used in the past. In managing your anger you work toward *not* having anger outbursts, temper tantrums, or violent reactions (abstinence). Abstinence means choosing not to do something. Instead you learn to assess or evaluate the problem that is generating your anger and take the necessary *anger action* in order to resolve the problem. In order to take the right anger action, you must know the warning signs and risk factors that show you are not dealing with your anger very well.

Pre-Cycle Risk Factors

If you take a moment to stand back and look at your anger from a distance, you will find that anger outbursts do not "just happen." You do not just simply hit somebody for no reason. Usually there is some early sign that you are becoming angry—that is, *risk factors* are present. Risk factors are events or emotions that push your buttons or set you up to be angry. They threaten your sense of self

Figure 9
A Model of the Anger Relapse Process

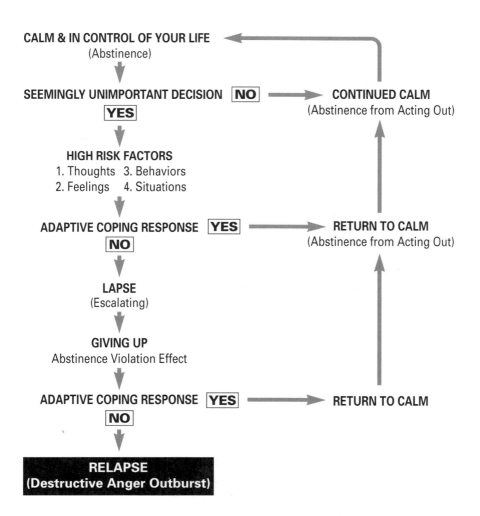

Anger Management and Relapse Prevention

control. They contribute to your "losing your cool." These risk factors are identified by many names—some writers refer to them as "early warning signals" or "road signs." All of these terms mean the same thing. *Risk factors* are the circumstances, situations, triggering events, thoughts, feelings, and behaviors that occur in your life and happen just before you begin to act in an angry manner.

Below is a list of common "general" or "pre-cycle" risk factors. They occur in your day-to-day life *before* you are in your anger cycle (*pre*-cycle), and they are warning signs that you are probably not managing your anger well. When you find yourself having a problem in any of these areas, it may be a warning that you are beginning to stuff your feelings and hold on to your anger. They show that you are in the Pretends To Be Normal phase of your anger cycle. Read through them and see how many apply to you.

FINANCIAL. When you hold onto your anger, you may find that you start to mismanage your money by not paying bills, spending money on alcohol or drugs, running up credit cards, etc. Mismanaging your money adds to your stress and results in your feeling angry and/or irritable.

EMPLOYMENT. When you are angry you may find that it affects your job. You may notice that you've gotten into a pattern of being late to or absent from work when you are holding onto anger. It may be that your job is one of your sources of *ongoing* anger. Take the time to look at your past closely. Before you had an angry outburst were you having problems at work? Did the boss "rake you over the coals" for something you did wrong? Did you begin to drink or use drugs on the job? Have you been getting involved in shop or office politics or rumors at your work place? Have you been regularly leaving work early or taking long lunches?

SOCIAL LIFE. Your anger can affect your social life, or it may be that your social life is part of the reason you are experiencing anger. If you have been carrying around your anger for a while, you are probably noticing that people are avoiding you, or making excuses not to get together. People don't usually like to spend time around individuals with an angry attitude, especially if you are acting out with violence. You may tend to isolate yourself from others and stay alone at home for days. Even if you have a wife and children, you may shut them out of your life by staring at the television, working in the garage, or yelling at them even when they have done nothing wrong, etc. You may pick arguments with other family members.

EDUCATION/TRAINING. Anger can affect the way you perform in school or in on-the-job training. If you are in some type of school system or vocational training, your grades may start to slip. You may start skipping classes or get angry at teachers for criticizing your homework assignments.

DRUGS AND ALCOHOL. Using alcohol and drugs has an impact on your ability to think and reason. It can affect your ability to use good judgement and common sense. Just before getting into violent situations, you might start using drugs or alcohol. You might experience a lot of anxiety trying to find money to spend on alcohol, you might start using drugs by yourself, even selling drugs. If you use drugs and alcohol a lot, it can lower your ability to be able to think clearly and act in a responsible way.

MARITAL/DATING. Just as anger can effect your social life, it can affect your ability to develop and/or maintain relationships with others. Before you acted in a violent manner, you might have started fights or become critical of your partner. You might have had arguments over sexual issues or either stopped having sex with your partner, or forced your partner to have sex.

LEISURE TIME. People who are angry don't usually spend free time being creative or enjoying themselves. You get "bored" and then wind up "looking for some action" and set yourself up to get into a fight. If you have any type of anger problem, an important sign occurs when you are unable or just not interested in occupying your spare time. If you find yourself preferring to watch TV for hours instead of doing anything else, it may be a signal that things are not right in your life. Some people turn to drugs or drinking simply as a method of passing the time. Some people drive aimlessly. In general, many people just have a lack of interest in anything.

HEALTH/PHYSICAL APPEARANCE. Holding onto anger can affect your health and/or result in neglecting your health and your physical appearance. Your health is likely to go downhill just prior to slipping into a violent cycle. You may not be as careful with your personal appearance; you may wear clothes that are dirty, missing buttons, not ironed properly, etc. You might find that you begin eating junk foods and do not look after yourself.

All of these characteristics are risk factors. Looking back at your own violent incidents and anger outbursts, which of these risk factors (or others that are not mentioned) are problem areas for you when you are not dealing very well with your anger or setting yourself up to act out? These signal you to take a close look at what is going on with your life right now.

Seemingly Unimportant Decisions (SUDs)

Whether or not we realize it, we make *Seemingly Unimportant Decisions* (SUDs) all the time. SUDs are decisions that appear to be reasonable and unrelated to your anger problem—but they have a direct impact on what you do later and what will happen to you. When you make these decisions, they don't seem like a big deal to you, and they don't seem to have anything to do with your anger cycle, but in fact they are very important. SUDs take you the next step toward your anger outburst. If you have a drinking problem, deciding to go to a bar when you are angry is an example of a SUD. Another example of a SUD is deciding to have a "serious talk with your wife" after having a bad day at work and during a time when you and your wife have had lots of problems.

If you have been angry with your wife and had a bad day at work, it is probably *not* a good time to sit down and have a serious talk. Making a decision to talk right then is probably a set up for an argument because you already are angry and have an attitude. This decision is an example of a SUD.

More Risk Factors

The risk factors outlined in the first part of this chapter occur *before* your anger acting-out cycle starts spinning. Once you have let yourself be *triggered* by something someone says or does or a particular situation or event, you are entering into your anger cycle. Once into your anger cycle there are more risk factors that keep threatening your sense of self control. Listed below are other possible risk factors divided into different types.

Some risk factors are thoughts, feelings, and events that probably began during your childhood and still influence the way you think (consciously or unconsciously), feel, and behave today. As an adult, you experience events and situations that remind you of experiences earlier in your life. Experiences most closely linked to anger problems include being physically, emotionally, or sexually abused as a child. Being physically pushed or beaten is physical abuse. Being told all the time that you are stupid and worthless is a form of emotional abuse. Being forced, tricked, or bribed to watch or participate in sexual acts in childhood is sexual abuse. These risk factors are never an excuse for acting out your anger violently, but they do *predispose* you toward having a lot of unresolved anger that you must now learn new ways to deal with. They are called *predisposing* risk factors.

Another type of risk factor is happening right now and has no apparent connection with your past. These risk factors are thoughts, feelings, and events in your life that trigger your anger cycle and move you from the **Pretends to Be Normal** phase into your **Build-Up** and **Acting Out** phases. Examples of these risk factors include being pushed around, being told what to do, being put down by others, having arguments with others, etc. These are called *precipitating* risk factors because they *precipitate* your anger, they crystallize or trigger your anger.

The third type of risk factor involves things that have been a problem in your life for a long time. They will probably continue to be a problem unless you make serious changes in your life, and sometimes these risk factors will still be a problem for you even then. These ongoing risk factors are thoughts, feelings, behaviors, and events that often help you maintain the **Pretends To Be Normal** phase of your anger cycle. Examples of this type of risk factors include unresolved anger, chronic alcohol and drug abuse, or a job with built-in stress. Each of these risk factors can include thoughts, emotional feelings, body sensations, behaviors, and situations (see Figure 10).

THOUGHTS. When you become angry you have a series of thoughts that link together with feelings and behaviors and support and maintain your anger. In having these thoughts you probably make a lot of *negative self-statements,* or *negative self-talk.* These thoughts usually feed your anger by distorting reality. Below is a list of the types of thoughts that go through the minds of people just before they act out their anger.

- *They think I'm not good enough.*
- *They are rejecting me.*
- *I'm stupid.*
- *I'm a failure.*
- *I'll make them pay!*
- *He/she deserves a good punch in the face.*
- *I'll show them!*
- *Nobody likes me.*
- *I deserve to feel sorry for myself.*
- *I'm right—they're all idiots.*
- *He/she can't tell me what to do!*
- *These people are doing that to me on purpose.*

EMOTIONS/FEELINGS. Anger is an emotion or feeling. Most people who experience the feeling of anger experience other feelings before or while the anger is developing. Frustration is one of the most common feelings that go along with anger. Feelings of rejection, helplessness, depression, inadequacy, embarrassment, fear, and resentment are also common. You may start to dwell upon your feelings as you get more and more angry, nearer to exploding.

BODY SENSATIONS. In addition to emotional feelings, you experience body sensations of anger arousal. These body sensations

Figure 10
High Risk Factors for Anger/Aggression

Risk Factors for Anger/Aggression*

PREDISPOSING (Early) RISK FACTORS	PRECIPITATING (Triggering) RISK FACTORS	PERPETUATING (Ongoing) RISK FACTORS
1. EMOTIONAL FEELINGS a. Numbness b. Fear	1. EMOTIONAL FEELINGS a. Frustration b. Rejection	1. EMOTIONAL FEELINGS a. Depression b. Low self-esteem
2. THOUGHTS a. Who cares? b. They're out to get me	2. THOUGHTS a. Right to act out with violence b. Distortions/errors	2. THOUGHTS a. Thinking errors b. Defense mechanisms
3. BEHAVIOR a. Isolation b. General anger /aggressiveness	3. BEHAVIOR a. High risks b. Isolation	3. BEHAVIOR a. Substance abuse b. Working too much
4. SITUATION a. Chaotic family b. Job stress	4. SITUATION a. Opportunity to act out b. PIG, urges to act out	4. SITUATION a. Arguments with others c. Threats
5. BODY SENSATIONS a. Anxiety b. Tensions	5. BODY SENSATIONS a. Face flushed b. Clenched teeth	5. BODY SENSATIONS a. Stomach ache b. Muscle tension

* Adapted with permission from Gray & Pithers, 1993.

are signs that your anger is building. Examples of body sensations are:

- Face becomes flushed
- Muscles become tense
- Veins in your neck pop out
- Clenched fists
- Gritting your teeth
- Knot in your stomach
- An "adrenaline rush" in your arms or chest

- Narrowed vision
- Feeling fear
- Shaking
- Headache
- Temples pulsing or pounding
- Breathing fast and shallow
- Nausea

BEHAVIORS. You usually begin to act differently when you are quickly becoming angry. If you ask others who know you well, they can usually describe very accurately the differences they see in the way you act when you're getting angry and the ways you usually behave when you're not. Examples of changes that other people can see in the way you behave include:

- Looking depressed
- Becoming more secretive
- Pacing the floor or chewing fingernails
- Staring at nothing (looking spaced out)
- Stuttering

- Avoiding eye contact
- Being extremely sarcastic
- Distorting information or lying
- Isolating from others
- Swearing a lot more than usual
- Covering up hurt or embarrassed feelings with laughter

SITUATIONS. Events and situations occur that trigger anger. Everyone has one or more "buttons" that other people can "push" to trigger anger. When you are being abused, put down, or your property is destroyed or stolen, you are likely to feel angry. As you increase your self-awareness you discover key situations that produce anger every time you experience them. These situations become automatic. If they happen, you automatically begin to feel angry. You must learn to avoid, escape from. or respond to these situations differently if you are going to control your anger. Examples include:

- Arguments with significant others: wife or girlfriend, boss, landlord
- Verbal fights at bars
- Abusing alcohol and drugs[2]
- Going to certain places
- Being around people who drink/abuse drugs
- Not getting enough sleep
- Being around people who always upset you
- Your job

Adaptive Coping Responses (ACRs)

The goal in learning anger management is to either "detect and deflect" or resolve anger before it becomes a problem for you. You can *detect* that your anger is building up by paying attention to your emotions, your body sensations, and your risk factors. By keeping an anger log you are learning to keep up your awareness about anger triggers and to correct the situation as soon as you detect that you are experiencing one of your risk factors. When you discover that you are experiencing a high risk factor you can *deflect* the possibility of an anger outburst by using an *adaptive coping response* (ACR) to avoid or escape the risk factor you have detected. Adaptive coping responses are the *interventions* you will use to keep yourself from getting to the **Anger Acting-Out** phase of your cycle. One adaptive coping response that you have already learned is taking a time out.

An adaptive coping response helps you assess each situation so you can avoid anger outbursts and acting out. ACRs are positive changes in your thoughts, feelings, and/or behaviors that help you deal with risk factors or avoid a *lapse*. ACRs may be general (such as talking it out with a friend when you are depressed or angry) or specific to certain situations (such as avoiding a risky situation by not going to bars).

[2]Some individuals have a strong negative reaction to taking drugs or using alcohol. They experience a personality change, like Dr. Jekyll and Mr. Hyde. When they abuse alcohol/drugs they become irritable and angry. You may have this problem if people refer to you as a mean drunk.

Consider for a moment that everything is going fairly well for you. During the course of your day a situation occurs that triggers your anger. You make a seemingly unimportant decision (SUD) to "ignore" the situation (but really you are stuffing your feelings about it). By doing so, you are experiencing a risk factor. Whether it is a thought, feeling, or behavior, in order to avoid an anger outburst or violent reaction, you must use an ACR. When you use adaptive coping responses you make it less likely that you will have an unwanted anger reaction, and you prevent your anger from escalating into a violent and hurtful outcome. Kevin's story illustrates the importance of SUDs and the possibilities for using ACRs.

Kevin allowed himself to get mad at his wife Julie one evening and made a SUD to go to the bar and drink with some buddies to chill out. While drinking Kevin moaned and groaned about his wife and how she didn't understand him. His buddies began to feed him more and more lines about how Julie didn't *really* care about him. His buddies' bitter words just mad him madder and madder.

As his anger grew, he thought about hurting Julie when he got home. The drinks lowered his inhibitions, affected his thinking, and let Kevin give himself permission to hurt Julie. His buddies reinforced his decision by saying that she "deserved" to be "put in her place" and that no "real man" would let his wife boss him around like that. It sounded to Kevin like his buddies were encouraging him to hit Julie in order to put her in her place.

When Kevin went home, he opened the door quietly, and just sat in the living room waiting for Julie to say something— anything—so he could start arguing again and then hit her in order to "prove" his "manhood." As the argument got more and more heated, Kevin felt his rage building until he smashed Julie in the mouth with his fist. When the cops came, he said, "She just wouldn't shut up—I just had to shut her up! She shouldn't be talking back at me like that anyway. She's my wife! I've got a right to discipline a disrespectful wife." The cops recognized that Kevin's distorted thoughts were typical of batterers, and Kevin spent the rest of the night in jail.

In reality no one gave Kevin permission to hit or hurt anybody or anything! Kevin *decided* to react with violence to this particular situation. An *adaptive coping response* (ACR) in this example would have been for Kevin to take a time out during his argument with Julie when he began to feel his anger coming on. He could have avoided the high-risk factor by not going to the bar. But even if he went to the bar, Kevin could have escaped the situation by leaving the bar when his drinking buddies began to feed his anger by supporting the distorted notion of "putting his wife" in her "place."

Another *adaptive coping response* would have been to leave the bar and go somewhere else, perhaps to the home of a good friend who would discourage Kevin from drinking and discuss appropriate ways to deal with his problems. Other possible ACRs for different situations include:

- Accept "no" for an answer
- Take a time out
- Remember you are a person of worth
- Ask for clarification (ask the person to explain)
- Respect the other person's position
- Accept whatever responsibility is yours
- Find something else to do
- Take a few deep breaths before reacting
- Be aware that you could be wrong in this case, and that being wrong isn't bad, just human
- Think of the other person's feelings in the situation
- Be aware that you need to control yourself because only you are responsible for your own actions

Maladaptive Coping Responses (MCR)

Maladaptive coping responses are "counter-productive"—they might get you some of what you think you want, but they do it in a harmful way. A *maladaptive coping response* is something that doesn't really work. Although it might *seem* to work at first, it usually just gets you into more trouble, usually by escalating the situation. Screaming obscenities at the driver who bumped your car pulling out of a parking space might *seem* to work because it intimidates the person who upset you, but it gets you into more trouble because it feeds your anger and might trigger you into a violent response. ***Maladaptive coping responses are the opposite of what you should do when you experience a risk factor or a lapse.*** MCRs are the ways you already think, feel, and behave that lead you closer to an angry or violent outburst. Examples include: drinking to solve problems (as Kevin did) or letting your anger escalate (that is, continuing to argue with someone, or letting others feed into your anger like Kevin did). An MCR allows you to move from the frying pan into the fire.

Lapses

Lapses occur when you experience or enter into a risk factor and *do not* use an adaptive coping response. They are even more likely to occur when you experience a risk factor and use a *maladaptive* coping response. (Remember, these are two different things: the first one is *not* doing the right thing that would keep you out of trouble; the second one is *doing* the thing that will get you deeper into your anger cycle and into trouble.) Lapses are emotions, fantasies, thoughts, and/or behaviors that are a part of your anger cycle and relapse pattern. They are not anger outbursts or aggressive episodes. They are the thoughts, feelings, and/or behaviors that occur just *before* you act out your anger. They set you up to act out. Lapses are **not** failures; in fact, they can be valuable learning experiences. Examples of lapses in an anger cycle might include the following:

- Picking up something you are likely to use to hit a person or throw, such as a stick, a cue ball, an ashtray, a rock, etc.
- Getting drunk or using drugs
- Continuing to think about the situation that made you angry
- Trying to pick a fight
- Looking for an argument
- Thinking "I'll show him" or "I'll teach her a lesson..."
- Not dealing with destructive feelings such as fear
- Letting others influence the way you think or your behavior
- Thoughts or plans to get back, get even, or hurt another person

If you are experiencing a risk factor and do not use an adaptive coping response, or *do* use a maladaptive coping response, you are likely to *lapse*.

Think back to Kevin. Since Kevin has a problem with alcohol, then drinking was a lapse. Going home and continuing to argue with Julie was also a lapse. When Kevin thought about hurting Julie and then planned how he would do it, he was lapsing again.

Giving Up (Abstinence Violation Effect or AVE)

Once you become aware that you have had a lapse, you experience feelings of hopelessness, uselessness, worthlessness. You give up on yourself and think, "I can never change, so I might as well go ahead and do the worst possible thing right now and get it over with." These feelings are called the *abstinence violation effect*. It is that feeling of "I might as well go ahead since I've already blown it." It's giving up on your efforts to change your thoughts, feelings, and behavior. When you experience the AVE, you may think that you have no willpower and no control over your life. You may think of yourself as a loser destined always to fail. You might also experience the *Problem of Immediate Gratification* (PIG, defined below). You are most likely to experience AVE if you believe that you will *never* lapse and if you then think that you are a failure when you eventually do. But when you are prepared in advance to deal with the AVE, you are much less likely to go on in your cycle to full relapse and anger acting out.

The first thing to remember is that *everyone* lapses. The first time you tried to ride a bicycle, you probably fell. But you got back on and tried again, and fell again. You tried again, and this time you rode a little further before you fell. Because you wanted so much to be able to ride the bicycle, you kept getting back on and trying again. You practiced and practiced until you could not only ride without falling, but you had learned to use the brakes and steer around the potholes and broken glass and other obstacles in your way.

Learning to intervene in your Anger Acting-Out cycle by using Relapse Prevention skills is like learning to ride a bicycle. At first you fall or lapse a lot. You might even relapse and have a violent outburst. But it's up to you to keep believing in yourself and your ability to learn and use new skills to deal with your anger. When you have a lapse, read this section again. Review your time out reminder card. Make a list of the thoughts, feelings, and behaviors that led to your lapse. Study the situation that triggered you so you will recognize it when it comes up again. Lapses are experiences for learning how to handle the situation better next time. Don't give up!

Even if you feel like giving up and have a relapse, you can start again. It all depends on how much you want to change your life so that *you're* in control of it and your anger is not.

Another thing you may find yourself doing in the AVE is blaming others for your problems. Instead of taking responsibility for what you have done or not done to cause yourself problems, you blame others for your misfortune, for making you angry, or for your not succeeding when you try to change.

The AVE is often your own worst enemy. Think back to Kevin. When Kevin was drinking and talking to his buddies, he was lapsing in several ways. At the time he was lapsing he was also experiencing the AVE. In the back of his mind he was thinking about how he had tried in the past to work things out with Julie and how those efforts just haven't worked. He thought that all of his previous good efforts are now "down the drain." When Kevin thought about hitting Julie, it brought up thoughts about having hurt her physically and verbally in the past. Since his attempts to change haven't worked, he thinks "Why bother, what's the use? Things will never change. This is the way that I am and the way that I will always be—I may as well just accept it and live with it!"

The **PIG** phenomenon occurs when you think only about how good it will feel to you to pick a fight, or get drunk, or do any other behavior that would be considered a lapse or a relapse for you. While you are thinking about how good it will feel, you are ignoring any consequences of your actions, such as your bruises or broken bones, the other person's feelings or bruises or broken bones, destruction of property, possible arrest, wasted money, hangovers, poor performance at work, and so on.

Leo's experience also shows how the AVE and the PIG lead to relapse, angry acting out, and serious consequences.

Leo *lapsed* when he went to the bar even though he knew he was feeling bad, humiliated, and angry. He had more lapses when he drank several drinks and started letting his earlier conversations influence the way he was thinking about Sandra. When Leo began to fantasize about taking advantage of Sandra sexually, that was another lapse. As he continued to fantasize about driving her to a secluded area and putting the "moves" on her, his lapses continued. By fantasizing about what he would do to her and how good it would feel (ignoring how Sandra might feel) Leo experienced the PIG phenomenon. Unfortunately, Leo had not learned how to intervene in his anger cycle.

You have just finished reading about the basic principles in the relapse prevention process. As you do the exercises for this chapter and practice your relapse prevention skills, you may want to refer to Figure 9, the "flow chart" diagram of the anger relapse process, and Figure 11 (next page), a combined anger cycle and relapse process diagram. They should help you understand the different aspects of RP described in this chapter. It may be worthwhile for you to read through this section again and refer to the diagrams to refresh your understanding of how your cycle works and where the relapse process fits in.

Leo was having a bad day at work. His boss embarrassed him in front of some co-workers, including Sandra, whom he had been wanting to ask out for a while now. On the way home, Leo was feeling sorry for himself and stopped at a bar for a few drinks he felt he deserved, since he was having such a bad day.

"I really need to get laid," Leo thought, "I deserve it." Leo noticed Sandra sitting a few tables away. He thought to himself, "The bitch has 'teased' me way too long." Earlier that week he had been talking with some other guys from work about some of the women in their shop. They talked about the women like pieces of meat, as body parts, as if they were objects instead of human beings with feelings. Now, at the bar, Leo thought, "I'll be a nice guy and offer her a ride home." But, at the same time he thought, "She can't escape from me in the car. I'll be in control. I'll make her do me good." He was arrested two days later for raping Sandra.

Figure 11
Anger Cycle With Relapse Process

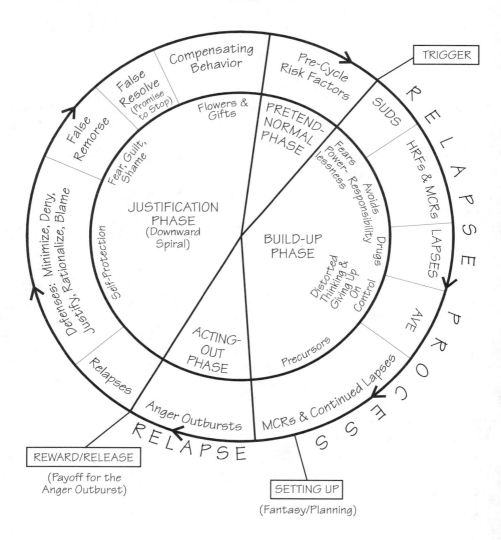

© 1994 Murray Cullen & Robert E. Freeman-Longo. Adapted from *A Structured Approach to Preventing Relapse*, ©1992, with permission from The Safer Society Program.

Chapter Eight Exercises

EXERCISE #8-1: Risk Factors

a) In your notebook make a list of your **pre-cycle** risk factors. Be as specific as you can and consider money, job, social life, education, use of drugs & alcohol, marital/dating relationship, leisure time, and health or physical appearance. List your thoughts, feelings, and behaviors that you experience with each risk factor.

b) Using the Risk Factor Worksheet on the next page as a model, make a copy in your notebook. List your risk factors. Include your thoughts, feelings, behaviors, body sensations, and situations. Your risk factors can be **predisposing** (early childhood), **precipitating** (triggering), or **perpetuating** (ongoing).

EXERCISE #8-2: SUDs

In your notebook, briefly describe three anger situations from your anger log. List the place each occurred, who was involved, and what you did. Write down the **Seemingly Unimportant Decisions** you made.

EXERCISE #8-3: ACRs

Using the same three anger situations, list some possible **adaptive coping responses** that you could have used to avoid acting out your anger. Remember to include thoughts and feelings as well as behaviors.

EXERCISE #8-4: MCRs

Still working on the same situations, in your notebook list the things you thought, felt, and did that were **maladaptive coping responses** (got you deeper into your anger cycle and closer to an anger relapse).

Anger Management and Relapse Prevention

Risk Factor Worksheet

Make a list of your Risk Factors in the spaces below:

RISKY
SITUATIONS
1. _____
2. _____
3. _____
4. _____
5. _____

RISKY
THOUGHTS
1. _____
2. _____
3. _____
4. _____
5. _____

RISKY
FEELINGS
1. _____
2. _____
3. _____
4. _____
5. _____

RISKY
BEHAVIORS
1. _____
2. _____
3. _____
4. _____
5. _____

RISKY BODY
SENSATIONS
1. _____
2. _____
3. _____
4. _____
5. _____

EXERCISE #8-5: Lapse

a) Write down at least three lapses that occurred in each of the three anger outburst situations you have been describing in this chapter's exercises. List thoughts and feelings as well as behaviors.

b) Make a list of the types of lapses you anticipate you will be faced with in the future. They may be examples of past lapses you have already experienced (for example, provoking a fight, feeling powerful and violent, escalating an argument), as well as lapses you have never experienced before but think you could possibly face in the future (not walking away if someone picks a fight with me, challenging my boss's authority).

EXERCISE #8-6: Giving Up (AVE)

a) In your notebook, describe a time when you gave up trying to change. It can be about controlling your anger or about another issue, such as quitting smoking. Remember to include your thoughts and feelings as well as your behavior. Don't forget the PIG (focusing on the payoff for your anger and ignoring the hurtful consequences).

b) Write examples of each type of AVE you have experienced in the past or are likely to experience in the future. Make sure to include examples for: 1) self-deprecation ("I'm worthless—I can't control my behavior"); 2) expecting to fail ("Nothing I do ever works out right—why bother"); 3) PIG Phenomenon ("It's gonna feel so good to hit him"); and 4) blaming others ("It's the lawyer's fault" "It's my wife's fault").

EXERCISE #8-7: Consequences

In these three situations you've been working on, list who got hurt. What got broken? What were the short-term and long-term effects of your anger outburst? Describe your thoughts, feelings, and behavior right after your anger outburst. Describe your thoughts, feelings, and behavior that helped you return to the **Pretends To Be Normal** phase.

EXERCISE #8-8: Resolution

For the same three situations, list at least three possible anger actions for each one that you could have taken to resolve the problem without aggression or violence.

EXERCISE #8-9: Relapse Prevention and My Anger Cycle

In this exercise you will make a diagram that combines your Anger Cycle with Relapse Prevention. Take one of the three situations you've been working on, and in your notebook, diagram the situation in the form of your anger cycle. Show your thoughts, feelings, and behaviors that move you from one part of your cycle to another. Show where you could intervene and list the interventions. While some interventions might not work, you can still intervene after you have lapsed! Explain your diagram to a friend, your therapist or group leader, or your spouse.

Chapter Nine
Interventions

This chapter addresses several methods you can use either to avoid the situations and events that trigger your anger or to reduce how much and how fast you let your anger build. If you are honest about wanting to manage your anger, control your life, and change the aggressive ways you have lived your life in the past, then you will spend a lot of time reading and reviewing this chapter.

As we mentioned in Chapter Eight, practice is what works in learning a new skill. You can never practice your intervention skills too much. If you have ever played football or basketball, or watched a team practice, you know that the players practice every play over and over and over and over and over and over again. They practice the play until it is beyond perfect, until it is beyond just being memorized, until it is just about automatic. The team members don't stop thinking, even when the play is so much a part of them. They think about when and where to use the play and how to adapt it when a slightly different situation arises.

To interrupt your anger cycle and make the changes that will put you in control of your life, you need to learn these interventions in the same way. If you do not practice these skills and use them, your anger problem will not change, and it will certainly not get any better. We want you to go beyond just learning these skills, we want you to over-learn them, eat-sleep-and-breathe them. Consider these skills your lifeline to quality living.

If you have not been keeping an anger log, you should begin one immediately. You will need the information on the log sheets in order to understand and learn the intervention skills. We will make several references to your anger journal or log as we review these interventions. These interventions are not introduced in any particular order, and you do not have to use them in the order that they are presented here. Everyone is different. What works for the other person may not work for you and vice versa. Try different interventions and see which ones work best for you. So, let's begin.

Coping Responses

In Chapter Eight you learned that adaptive coping responses help prevent your anger from building. We wrote that there were two types of adaptive coping responses; general coping responses and specific coping responses.

General coping responses improve the quality of your life. They include managing anger, improving your relationship skills, reducing stress, learning and using problem-solving skills, and changing your lifestyle and habits so they no longer support your aggressive behaviors and tendencies. General adaptive coping responses help you *prevent* problems.

Specific coping responses deal with your personal risk factors and lapses. They include learning to avoid events and situations that trigger your aggressive behavior (*stimulus control*), avoiding high risk factors (the easiest), escaping from risk factors (the hardest), developing and using specific coping methods for a particular problem, changing the way you think, learning ways to prevent the PIG and the AVE from getting to you, and contracts (discussed later in this chapter). Adaptive coping means not giving up on yourself when the going gets tough.

Avoidance

One of the first tasks in learning to manage your anger is to avoid the situations you know will trigger it. This is where looking at your journal sheets and studying your trigger patterns come in handy. If you notice repeated triggers that get your anger going, try to avoid them. Michael's approach demonstrates.

Escape Strategies

Sometimes, no matter how well you have planned, you cannot avoid situations and events that get you angry because you do not see them coming. When you cannot avoid triggering events, another useful intervention is to *escape* situations and events that are triggering your anger. Taking a time out is one way to escape situations and events that trigger your anger. Another escape strategy is to postpone a situation that you know tends to anger you until you can better prepare yourself to deal with it. Neal (see his story on page 125) found this to be useful in his job.

> Michael has been working hard on controlling his anger. He has decided he is tired of being arrested for fighting. After charting his anger episodes for over a month, Michael noticed several triggers he could avoid. Two of his triggers were related. First, he noticed that when he visited his girlfriend Ellen, and she was drinking, they always got into an argument. Next he discovered when they argued he would usually get angry and leave her house and go to a local bar. The bar catered to a rough crowd and Michael logged that he got into fights there more than once, usually when some guy who had too much to drink said something to challenge or belittle him. To avoid these anger triggers Michael decided that he would immediately leave Ellen's house if she was drinking or if she began to drink. Michael told her of his decision at a time when she was sober, so she would understand what he was saying. He also realized that going to bars and drinking set him up to get angry and possibly get into a fight. Michael decided to go for a long walk or work on his woodcarving project instead of going to a bar.

Using a Decision Matrix

One way of helping you avoid getting into your anger cycle is to use a decision matrix, such as the one in Figure 12. Using a decision

Figure 12
Decision Matrix

	SHORT-TERM CONSEQUENCES		LONG-TERM CONSEQUENCES	
	POSITIVES	NEGATIVES	POSITIVES	NEGATIVES
ANGER ACT OUT	Release of emotions -Anger -Frustration Feel powerful	Hurt Julie Go to jail	None	Still has anger Has hurt Julie and lost her trust Arrest record
ANGER ACTION	Does not hurt Julie Does not go to jail	May still feel -Frustration -Anger	Resolves problems with Julie and feels good about self for managing anger	None

©1994 Murray Cullen & Robert E. Freeman-Longo. Adapted from *A Structured Approach to Relapse Prevention*, © 1992 Safer Society Program.

matrix helps you weigh the positive and negative aspects of getting angry. This is done by looking at both the short term and long term positive and negative outcomes of entering your anger act-out cycle versus using your anger action cycle.

For example, look at Kevin's situation on page 110. The short-term positive result of Kevin's anger outburst was the immediate release of his emotions (anger, frustration, rage). The short-term negative consequences of his anger out-burst were hurting Julie and spending the night in jail. The short-term positive aspects of using his anger action plan might have been not hurting Julie and avoiding jail, and the short-term negative consequences might have been continuing to feel frustrated and angry at Julie.

There are no long-term positive consequences for Kevin entering into his anger act-out cycle because the problems that caused his anger (a short fuse and mismanaged anger) have not been resolved. The long-term negative consequences for entering into his anger cycle and hitting Julie are hurting Julie's feelings, losing her trust, and having an arrest record. The long-term positive consequences for Kevin using his anger action plan would be working out his problems with Julie and learning to control and express his anger in a healthy way. There

Neal's job as a carpenter required him to work with Orson, another carpenter for the same construction company. Sometimes in building or remodeling jobs, Neal and Orson would disagree on how to hang a cabinet or trim out the siding. Orson would suggest one way and Neal the other.

The first few times this disagreement happened, Neal got angry and yelled at Orson, his face turning beet red. He even called Orson a "dumb, stubborn SOB," and stalked off to work by himself, kicking tools and scrap pieces of lumber out of his way.

After the crew boss warned him that this kind of behavior was unacceptable on the job site, Neal realized he had to find a way to escape the situation before he got angry. Neal discovered that if he drew up a diagram, Orson would often agree with him after all. Neal learned to escape arguments with Orson by suggesting they come back to the problem later on or the next day. Neal would then take the time to draw a diagram to show Orson. If Orson liked the diagram they would build it Neal's way. If Orson did not like Neal's diagram, they would build it Orson's way. In taking this extra step, Neal was able to escape from the situations that would trigger his anger.

are no long-term negative consequences for Kevin's using his anger management plan.

Communicate and Check Things Out

When the anger you experience is related to an event or situation involving other people, one key to fixing the problem is good communication. You need to learn how to *talk* (not yell) *and* to *listen* (not tune out the other person). Talking and listening work best when you don't let yourself react emotionally right away. Take a deep breath. Try to think about where the other person is coming from. Probably the other person is not trying to hurt your feelings or insult you. Communication is a process of give and take. Some of the skills you need for good communication include *active listening, checking out the information, asking for clarification, using "I" statements,* and *being assertive.*

Active listening is a simple but important way of communicating that many people ignore. Active listening means to listen closely to what the other person says. Let the person finish what he or she is saying. Don't interrupt or cut the person off. Listening gives you the chance to hear all of the information. It is pretty hard to listen well when you are thinking about what you are going to say back to the person or when you interrupt. Active listening also involves making sure you have correctly understood what the person is saying by summarizing what you heard and asking for correction if you have misunderstood. Do not interpret what the other person said, just summarize.

If you expect others to listen to you, to respect your feelings, and to listen to what you have to say, you must be willing to listen to others in the same way. You, like others, may get angry because you do not take the time to listen to what others have to say.

Check out the information you have heard. It may be untrue, it may be inaccurate, it may be distorted or blown way out of proportion. If you are not absolutely sure about what you have heard, don't make assumptions. Take the time to check it out.

Give yourself permission to be open to feedback. You are not perfect and you, like the rest of us, make mistakes. Because you are not perfect, you are not necessarily the best judge of your behavior. None of us is. Others often have a much better picture of how we behave and how we conduct ourselves. They observe what we say and what we do from day to day. If others offer you feedback, take the time to listen to it and absorb it. Your best friends will be honest with you. They will offer you honest criticism and point out your inconsistencies, as well as reminding you of what they like about you.

If you do not understand something you have been told, or if you do not understand feedback from someone else, *ask for clarification.* There is nothing wrong with saying you did not understand what someone else has said, or that you want the person to repeat what he or she said. It's perfectly all right to ask questions. People who are smart and have knowledge learn by asking questions. If you don't ask questions you may not get all the information.

When you address others, *use "I" statements.* If you are upset, you will gain others' respect and decrease your level of anger by personalizing what you say. Statements such as "I feel hurt when people yell at me" or "I feel put down when people make fun of me" are not threatening or accusing. Accusations such as "you hurt me," "you make me mad," or controlling statements such as "stop making fun of me" often escalate anger situations.

Learn to *assert your feelings* appropriately. Assertiveness is not being aggressive or passive. Assertiveness is standing up for your rights without affecting the rights of others. If you feel you are not assertive, try to read materials on being assertive or take a course in assertiveness training.

Labeling Escalates Your Anger

Labeling situations or people can set up destructive patterns of behavior and feed your anger. Often we have specific feelings attached to labels we place on people, places or objects. For example, have you ever met someone who had the same name as someone you didn't like? What sometimes happens in this situation is that you take an initial dislike to the person you were just introduced to because that person has the same name as someone from your past that you dislike.

Labeling also tends to generalize. In other words, labeling puts similar things into the same category. If you are afraid of dogs because you were bit by a German Shepherd, you may come to fear all German Shepherds or in some cases *all* dogs. This is because the label of "bad" or "dangerous" was placed on "dog" instead of on a German Shepherd named Killer. The same process can unfairly label people by whether they are male, female, black, white, brown, Hispanic, Asian, French, ex-convicts, civilians, straight, gay, able-bodied, or handicapped. Because you had a bad (or good) experience with one person in the category, doesn't mean that the same thing will happen with all people of that category.

When you label someone, you make certain assumptions about the person that may or may not be true. Labeling interferes with communication because people who label others think they already know what "his kind" or "her kind" are going to say. Labeling people, lumping them into a large group and making assumptions about them, makes it way too easy for you to escalate an anger situation by thinking you can "mind read" what they're thinking about you.

Mind Reading Makes Things Worse

One of the things you may do that feeds into your anger is "mind reading." Mind reading is saying in your head what you think another person is going to say, or what you think (or are afraid) the other person "really" thinks. You expect the person to say something negative and, in your mind, you may actually believe that the person has said it, even though she or he has not said it at all. Quint did this a lot.

Avoid Blaming Others

One of the most common things people do when they are angry is blame others or situations for their misfortune and anger. If you listen to others talking about their problems or their angers, usually you will hear them blaming their relatives, their coworkers or supervisors, their parents, the government,

> Quint has been married to Gina for five years. They have been arguing a lot over the past six months. Once when Gina got really angry she called Quint "stupid and good for nothing" (something Quint heard a lot from his mother when he was growing up). Over the past few weeks Quint has hit Gina as soon as they got into an argument. Quint was arrested, placed on probation, and ordered by the judge to enter counseling. While in counseling, Quint learned that he hit Gina because he began to "mind read" and became furious. As soon as they began to argue, Quint expected Gina to call him "stupid and good for nothing." To avoid hearing this and having his feelings hurt, Quint would hit Gina as soon as they began to argue in order to stop her from saying anything.

the lawyer, the judge, the probation or parole officer, their victims, society, or anyone else they can think of. When you put blame somewhere else you set yourself up as a victim. Victims are usually angry because someone has done something to hurt them or they have been the victim of something they cannot control.

If someone has done something wrong to you or an event has occurred that you could not control, then you have the right to be angry as a victim. If, however, something happened to you because you *chose* to put yourself in a situation, your anger at the situation is probably not justified. If you were the victim of someone's unprovoked attack, then you have the right to be angry as a result of being victimized. In these cases, you can honestly and rightfully blame another or a situation for your pain, hurt, and/or misfortune. But even when someone else (even God) appears to be responsible for what happened to you, only you are responsible for how you respond. You can keep yourself in the blame game, or you can work on healing yourself from the pain you felt when you were hurt. You can find ways to help yourself and others, or you can stay a victim. That is one choice that is always up to you.

On the other hand, if you brought on the problem you are experiencing, the only person responsible for your predicament is yourself. If you speed by going 70 miles an hour in a 55 mile per hour zone, it is not the law, the police, or the road that is the problem. You are responsible because you made a clear and deliberate choice to speed, knowing that you could get a ticket.

If you go skiing in a posted avalanche zone against the advice of the ski patrol and get injured by an avalanche, you are responsible for your fate. The snow, the mountain, the weather, and God are not to blame.

Blaming can be dangerous. It lets you escalate your anger when you don't place responsibility where it belongs.

Changing Negative Thinking

Your thinking is one of the most important areas for you to work on if you are trying to change your behavior and control your anger. Changing your thinking can change everything else about how you relate to the world. In order to control your anger you will have to change the way you think about your anger. Think back to Chapter Seven with the information you learned about your anger cycle, and to Chapter Eight with the information you learned about your anger relapse process. Your anger cycle and anger relapse process consist of thoughts, feelings, and behaviors.

When we discussed the communication process above, we talked about active listening. We discussed that if you are going to change the way you think, you must be open to new information. To get new information, you must be willing to listen to others.

In order to listen, you must first clear your head. Clearing your head means learning to turn off the typical thoughts ("old tapes") you have had for years about anger, your beliefs about why you become angry, and your beliefs about what gets you angry. You must also stop "mind reading." Redd's anger pattern is a good example.

Learning to ignore the old tapes of distorted information that you learned when you were younger helps you begin to think about situations differently. It opens up the avenue for you to communicate with others. Listening to old tapes (old thoughts) is more likely to lead you down the familiar road of fighting,

Redd argues with his wife Felicia a lot of the time. Whenever she suggests that Redd do something, he gets angry. He tells himself, "Dammit, Felicia is bossing me around again." Redd hates to be told what to do, so when Felicia suggests something, Redd's old tapes start to play. He tells himself, "Women always stick their noses where they don't belong" (something his father always said), and "They are always trying to run my life." In reality, Felicia is just trying to help Redd by making suggestions. Felicia has no interest in running Redd's life or telling him how to run it.

yelling, screaming, name calling, hitting, and destructive acting out.

Old tapes are often filled with imperative words. Imperatives are words that make what you are saying sound like commands, orders, do's, don'ts, and obligations. Examples of imperatives are the words **should, must, always,** and **never**. Examples of old tapes that you may hear in your mind include:

- "You'll *never* amount to anything!"   • "You *always* screw things up."
- "You *should* have done it my way."   • "You *must* do it my way."

Imperatives are words that sound controlling or threatening. Words that sound controlling and threatening often trigger anger or escalate it.

In Chapter Five we discussed defense mechanisms. Your defense mechanisms are distortions in your thinking. They are road blocks to your treatment and the change process. One of the things you can do as you begin to work on changing your thinking is to begin lowering your defenses. When you find yourself becoming defensive stop and check out your thinking. Ask yourself why you are in a defensive posture. Usually, your defensiveness is a result of irrational fears and thoughts about what you think may happen. If you are serious about changing your life and managing your anger, you will have to stop defending the thoughts, feelings, and behaviors that feed your anger.

Honesty: Acknowledging Your Part of the Problem

One of the problems people have when they are angry is not being able to admit that they might be wrong. This is often a result of old tapes which tell them that if they are wrong they are bad, or if they are wrong they are worthless. If you are stuck in your anger you will have a harder time acknowledging that you have a problem. The best thing to do when you recognize that you have a problem is to take responsibility for your problem and admit it to yourself and others who are involved. Being honest with yourself and others is a major intervention in your anger cycle and your relapse process. It is one of the best ways to deal with ongoing risk factors.

Honesty is the only way you can live a healthy life and use interventions to control your anger. Without a basic commitment to honesty you end up lying. Small lies lead to big lies. For example, an alcoholic, a sex offender, or a wife beater who says he is going to change without first making a basic commitment to be honest has already short-circuited the change process. Being honest means that you can tell the truth about what you have done in the past and what you are doing now. It means being honest with yourself and everyone else with whom you come into contact. If you think you can be honest with yourself and lie to others you are mistaken.

Take Responsibility for Your Behavior

The road to change is taking responsibility for the change process. Only you can change who you are and what you do. You must be willing to look honestly at your problems, ways of thinking, old habits, weaknesses, and imperfections. You are responsible for the success of your treatment.

Responsibility means that you take ownership of the bad things you have done as well as your good accomplishments. It means you are persistent at changing your behavior. You continue to work hard in your treatment and not give up.

Taking responsibility and owning your negative behaviors is often a real relief. Trying to hold up a perfect, always justified, never wrong image to the world creates an incredible burden, a weight that is hard to hold. Letting go of that image and no longer having to support its weight frees up a lot of energy for you to just be human instead of some kind of superman. It's a relief to just be able to be you in your most honest self, in control of your life without trying to control anyone else's.

Remember, too, that owning or taking responsibility for a negative behavior doesn't mean that you are bad. Your behavior is different from who you are as a person. You, as a person, are generally good. Good people may do hurtful things at times. It is your hurtful behavior that you are working on changing by acknowledging how it affects others.

Anger Action

As we discussed in Chapter Seven, part of changing your cycle of anger is turning your anger out-bursts and acting-out behaviors into *anger action*. That is, you direct your anger in a positive, productive direction to resolve the problem. Instead of escalating your anger, you work towards fixing the problem. As the saying goes, "If you're not part of the solution, you're part of the problem."

Taking anger *action* means you are part of the solution. In some cases you may find that taking anger action is engaging in a "pro-social" activity. That is, you might find yourself doing something that helps society by taking anger action against something that bothers you. Examples of pro-social activities are happening in the world around you on a daily basis. People are angry about crime. As a result they start neighborhood crimewatch groups. People are angry about pollution, or the littering at the town park or their favorite beach. They take anger action by forming groups and committees to clean up the environment, or they organize a community cleanup day, or perhaps they meet with town or state officials.

Steve and his wife Helen have argued for years over money. Most of the time they were finding that they couldn't pay all of their monthly bills. They were getting deeper and deeper into debt on their charge cards and/or pulling money out of their savings account just for regular bills. Each time they argued, the argument escalated to the point where both of them yelled. Steve usually got so angry he stormed out of the house. One day, they began arguing and Helen suggested that they stop arguing, get into the car, and go down to the office supply store and buy a home finance planning book. Steve stopped and thought about her suggestion and agreed that it was a good idea.

After tracking their finances for a month, they were able to see where they were overspending money. Steve was spending over $100.00 per month on radio controlled planes, parts, controllers, batteries, magazines, and entry fees for competitions. Helen was spending about that much on gardening books, supplies, and plants. They agreed to spend less on these two items and to stop charging anything on their credit cards. The next three months showed that they could meet their monthly expenses. As a result of balancing their budget, they stopped arguing so much.

If you take a close look at the events and situations that trigger your anger, you will find that in the majority of cases, you can take anger action to resolve the problem. Steve's situation is a good example.

Use Humor When Appropriate

Having a good sense of humor goes along way in combating anger and a bad attitude. People who are generally free from living angry lives maintain a good sense of humor. Sometimes the best response to situations that anger us is to look at the humorous side of things. In other instances, the use of humor can help break angry response patterns in our lives. In the example on the next page, Ted learned that humor helped to break the tension he often felt with Vinny on the job.

Part of using humor is discovering how it works for you. If you know that a good joke or someone pointing out how silly you look can break your angry thoughts, let your coworkers or friends know that it is okay to do that. Try to find the humor in situations when they begin to get too heavy.

Rest & Relaxation

Sometimes when you are under a lot of pressure and stress, things get tense. When things get tense, the tension may trigger your anger. Old fashioned "Rest & Relaxation" (R&R) may be exactly what you need. This is especially true if you have been working very hard or for long hours on a project. Long intense days often result in not eating and sleeping properly. Lack of sleep and poor nutrition affect your mood. It's OK to work hard as long as you take the time to play hard. Having fun can be relaxing.

You will need to look at your own daily patterns to determine if you are taking good care of your personal health. Research indicates that diet, rest, and exercise play an important and necessary role in how you feel, your level of irritability, and how well you cope with your emotions, especially anger.

Ted and Vinny are roofers and have their own business. When the job wasn't going well or a problem developed, Vinny would get uptight and angry really easy. One day Vinny was having a problem repairing a gutter that had fallen. As his anger built up, he began cursing, complaining about how things never go right, throwing things around, and talking about going out and getting drunk after work. Last time this started happening, Ted looked over at Vinny and cracked a joke about Ted winding up in the gutter as a drunk if he didn't fix the gutter. Vinny almost fell off his ladder from laughing so hard. By cracking the joke, Ted was able to break Vinny's tension and anger. He then helped Vinny hang the gutter back up.

One of the easiest ways to begin relaxing is to practice deep breathing. When you get angry, your breathing becomes more rapid and shallow. As you get angrier your body becomes more tense. Thus, it is impossible to be relaxed and angry at the same time. If you focus on relaxing and deep breathing, it will help reduce your anger level.

Interventions

135

Count Backwards

As we described earlier, anger is a chain of thoughts, feelings, and behaviors that result in a cycle of anger. If you begin to break the links in the chain, the cycle can be broken. One way to break the thoughts you are having that feed your anger is to change them. A simple way of breaking your thought pattern and stopping your anger thoughts is to simply count backwards from 100. If you have the opportunity, you may want to combine both deep breathing and relaxation with counting backwards from 100.

The real key is *just do something different!* Stand on your head, do push-ups, walk like a duck, put your thumbs on the sides of your head and waggle your fingers while making a silly face, anything that breaks up your anger pattern and helps you not escalate a tense situation into an anger outburst.

Personal Interests

When you work long and hard you need to balance the work with having fun. Activities such as hobbies, listening to music, joining clubs and organizations, playing sports, and so forth, offer you a balance in your life. Having personal interests can help to temporarily take your mind off the day-to-day problems you are dealing with that may be causing you to be tense and irritable and let your anger build.

Anger Contracts

Sometimes we need special tools to help us accomplish tasks in our lives. You need a hammer to drive a nail, a shovel to dig a hole, a screwdriver and directions to put together a piece of furniture, and a road map to get to someplace where you've never been before. You may find it useful and a good guide to develop an anger contract for managing your anger.

Anger contracts can be a one-page (or shorter) description of how you plan to work on managing your anger. Once you write one up, it is like have a personal road map to change your life. You can modify your anger contract as you improve your anger management skills, or if new and different situations arise. Figure 13 on the next page is an example of an anger contract you may want to use as a model in developing an anger contract for yourself.

Using Imagery

Imagery is using your imagination. Some people refer to it as fantasy or seeing something "in your mind's eye." Using imagery is a simple and pleasant way to help yourself relax. To use imagery, find a quiet, relaxing, peaceful place to practice this intervention. A lounge chair is ideal if you have one.

To use imagery, either recline your chair or lie down flat. Close your eyes and begin to think about a pleasant place. This place might be a favorite vacation spot, a secret fishing hole, or a place you have seen in a picture. Try to bring that image up in your mind. Imagine the trees, the rolling hills, the water, the blue sky, or whatever you imagine this place to look like.

Continue to visualize this place in your mind's eye and then imagine yourself in that place doing something that is fun and relaxing. In your imagery, let yourself stay in that spot, doing that relaxing activity (reading, fishing, watching clouds, or whatever) for at least 5 minutes. As you get more used to using imagery for relaxation, gradually let yourself stay there a little longer each time until you're up to 15 or 20 minutes. This sort of imagery is very useful in achieving relaxation.

Another important (but not relaxing) way to use imagery is called *consequential imagery*. In consequential imagery, you imagine yourself experiencing a negative *consequence* for your anger. For example, if you are angry with someone and feel like hitting him or her, you would create a negative image in your mind's

Figure 13
Anger Contract

NAME ___Jordan Axelrod___

EFFECTIVE DATE___May 15___ **UPDATE** ___June 15___

I will review my anger contract every Sunday evening and revise as necessary.

ANGER TRIGGERS: Argue with wife, Supervisor disciplines me in front of others.

RISK FACTORS: (THOUGHTS) Thinking others are trying to put me down, thinking others are trying to make me look bad, thinking people are out to get me. (FEELINGS) Frustrated, put down, disrespect, rage. (BEHAVIORS) Drinking, provoking fights, hitting others, throwing things. (PHYSICAL AROUSAL) Increased heart beat, flushed face, muscle tension.

When I feel myself getting angry I will use one or more of the following coping responses: •Take a time out. •Walk on the beach. •Deep breathing or relaxation exercises.

After using a coping response I will return to the event or situation and do one or more of the following: •Talk to the person I was having an argument with. •Go back and work on the project I was getting frustrated with. •Get a third (neutral) person to help resolve the problem I was having with the other person. •Ask for help in resolving the problem.

If I effectively deal with my anger and do not engage in an outburst, anger reaction, or violent/aggressive act, I will: •Spend an extra hour working on my hobby this week. •Reward myself with a pizza.

ANGER ACTION: To avoid the problem that triggered my anger from happening again I will: •Identify what started the argument and correct the problem. •Practice better listening skills and assertiveness skills. •Ask for a job reassignment. •Review my journal and look for similar patterns.

If I am not successful in managing my anger and I have an anger reaction, act-out, or become violent and/or aggressive, my consequences are: •Repair or replace any items or property I have destroyed. •Apologize for my behavior to the person with whom I argued. •Do a favor for the person with whom I became angry. •Spend two extra hours this week on learning to manage my anger.

© 1994, Murray Cullen & Robert E. Freeman-Longo

eye. That negative image might be the person telling you she or he never wants to see you again, being arrested and going to jail, or being sentenced to prison because you have assaulted someone or raped someone. This technique can be most useful when you find yourself being excited by anger thoughts of wanting to beat someone up, etc.

You can also use imagery to review problem-solving strategies in your mind. Picture the last time something happened that angered you. Think of what you did that helped you solve the problem. *Briefly* reviewing (but not brooding or dwelling on) what you did that made the problem worse can help you remember what *not* to do the next time. Mentally rehearse how you would assertively and appropriately deal with the event or situation that might trigger your anger again.

What Calms Me Down When I Am Angry?

Each of us knows the little secrets about ourselves and the specific keys to parts of us that others may not understand. For example, you know what part of your body is the most ticklish, or that you are not ticklish at all. You know what sorts of statements hurt your feelings more than others. You probably also know what calms you down when you are the most angry or upset.

You can better manage your anger by doing a couple of simple tasks. First, make a list of the things you know or believe can help you calm down and manage your anger. The list should include both things you can do for yourself and things others can do to help you. Once you have developed this list, you can begin practicing the things you can do for yourself immediately. Your list may include some of the interventions (such as deep breathing, relaxation, time outs, and so on) you have learned so far.

The other thing you can do is share with coworkers, close friends, and family members the list of what others can do help calm you down. Share the list only with people you are close to who will use them in a positive way to help you.

Calming Others

Other people are no different from you. They have anger triggers and specific interventions that work to calm them down when they become angry. If you find yourself in a situation where someone else has an anger problem, you may be able to use interventions to help calm the other person down. Usually, this involves practicing good communication skills (especially active listening), and being careful not to escalate the situation. A good saying to keep in mind when you find someone else losing control and getting angry is, "Behave with others the way you wish they would behave with you."

Establishing A Support System

It is extremely important for you to develop a support system and network of people who will help you work on changing your behavior. This part of Relapse Prevention is called **External Management**. A good support system, together with carefully reading and doing the exercises in this book, using other materials on anger management, and practicing interventions, will help you manage your anger and avoid destructive anger outbursts. Your support system consists of people you trust. It can include family, friends, relatives, co-workers, clergy, a probation or parole officer, a therapist, and others. Organizations that may be part of a good support system for you could include 12-Step groups such as Alcoholics Anonymous, Narcotics Anonymous, Adult Children of Alcoholics; religious groups; service clubs; or other organizations.

As you work on anger control, remember that there's no shame in asking for help from others, even when you might feel a little embarrassed. If you have a hard time asking for help, you may need to go back and check some of your old tapes. Has someone in your past called you stupid or put you down for not knowing something? Have you been shamed or made fun of for asking questions? If so, you will have to work on getting rid of the old tapes. The people in the world with the most and usually the best information are the ones who ask questions and listen carefully. There is nothing wrong in asking for help or information.

As a final reminder of all the interventions you have learned, we found the phrase "CHARMING BLACK BEARS" (see Figure 14). Bears are known to be pretty grumpy and cantankerous. It might even be said that some bears have an anger problem, since they growl at everybody and might attack at the slightest provocation. That's why it's important that these are *charming* bears. You will be less grumpy and less angry when you remember and use your interventions in your anger cycle.

Figure 14
Charming Black Bears

In order to help you remember all of the interventions we have discussed, make a wallet card carrying the phrase **"CHARMING BLACK BEARS,"** and the words each letter stands for:

C	=	**Coping responses**
H	=	**Humor**
A	=	**Avoiding risk situations**
R	=	**Relaxation exercises**
M	=	**Mind reading doesn't work**
I	=	**Interests and hobbies help**
N	=	**New thinking to replace old tapes**
G	=	**Go take a "Time Out"**
B	=	**Blaming others doesn't work**
L	=	**Labeling others doesn't work**
A	=	**Acknowledge there's a problem**
C	=	**Communicate and check things out**
K	=	**Keep practicing interventions**
B	=	**Breathe deep and relax**
E	=	**Escape high risk situations**
A	=	**Anger action, not anger outbursts**
R	=	**Responsible thinking and behavior**
S	=	**Situation Perception Training**

Chapter Nine Exercises

EXERCISE #9-1: Avoiding Angry Outbursts

In your notebook, list three of your anger triggers. Next to each situation or event that triggers your anger, list three ways you can plan ahead to avoid the situation or event.

EXERCISE #9-2: Escape Strategies

Using the same three triggers, list three ways you can escape from each situation if you weren't able to avoid it.

EXERCISE #9-3: ACRs

Make a copy of the Coping Responses Worksheet on page 145 in your notebook. In the left hand column, list as many of your high risk factors as you can think of (at least five, one of each type). In the right hand column, for each type of risk factor list at least two general coping responses and two specific coping responses that would help you avoid a relapse into a destructive anger outburst.

EXERCISE #9-4: My Anger Contract

In your notebook or on a separate piece of paper, write up your own anger contract (go back and look over Figure 13 to remind yourself what it should contain). In your contract identify your anger triggers, risk factors, coping responses, and anger actions. Share your contract with your group, counselor, friend, or spouse.

EXERCISE #9-5: Relaxation

List three different ways you can help yourself relax when you feel yourself getting angry. Beside each relaxation technique, describe how you would use that method in a specific anger situation or event. For example, "When I feel myself getting angry sitting in traffic jams, I can . . . "

EXERCISE # 9-6: Relapse Prevention.

Using the RP worksheet on page 146 as a model for a similar page in your notebook, review all of your risk factors and coping responses. Revise and update your Relapse Prevention Plan as needed every week for the next month to be sure your plan is working for you.

Coping Responses Worksheet

NAME _____

DATE _____ **SHEET NUMBER**_____

1. ANGRY FEELINGS/AGGRESSIVE BEHAVIORS

RISKY SITUATION (Trigger) _____

Pre-Assault Risk	**Coping Strategies**
Risky SUDs _____	Good Decisions _____
_____	_____
_____	_____
Risky Thoughts _____	Thoughts _____
_____	_____
_____	_____
Risky Feelings _____	Feelings _____
_____	_____
_____	_____
Risky Behaviors _____	Behaviors _____
_____	_____
_____	_____
Risky Justifications _____	Corrective Responses _____
_____	_____
_____	_____

2. HOW OTHERS CAN RECOGNIZE MY ANGER

What I Say _____
Body Language _____

Relapse Prevention Worksheet

NAME _____

DATE _____ **SHEET NUMBER** _____

RISKY SITUATION (Trigger) _____

Present Risk Situation	**New Coping Strategy**
SUDs _____ _____	Good Decision _____ _____
Thoughts_____ _____	Thoughts_____ _____
Feelings_____	Feelings_____
Behaviors _____ _____	Behaviors _____ _____
Thoughts_____ _____	Thoughts_____ _____
Feelings_____	Feelings_____
Behaviors _____ _____	Behaviors _____ _____
Thoughts_____ _____	Thoughts_____ _____
Feelings_____	Feelings_____
Behaviors _____ _____	Behaviors _____ _____

Discussed with _____ **Title** _____

Conclusion
Relapse Prevention: A Way of Life

In closing, we would like to congratulate you on reading this book and completing the exercises. If you have read the material and taken the exercises seriously, you are on the road to controlling your anger. Interventions work—but only when you practice and use them every day in real-life situations. Remember that you can intervene in your anger cycle anytime, even when you have lapsed and are on your way toward a relapse or destructive anger outburst. By using your new thinking and your new interventions, you can prevent the PIG and your anger from running your life. As time goes on, it will become easier and easier to avoid destructive anger outbursts. And if you slip, even years from now, these skills will be there waiting for you to use in helping you once more manage your anger and control your life. We wish you the best in your recovery from destructive anger and in your new way of life.

Murray Cullen
Hampton, NB, Canada

Robert E. Freeman-Longo
Brandon, VT

Appendix A
Anger Log Sheet

NAME _____

DATE _____ **SHEET NUMBER** _____

1. DAY AND DATE OF TRIGGERING EVENT		
2. WHAT I THOUGHT		
3. MY PHYSICAL SENSATIONS		
4. MY EMOTIONAL FEELINGS		
5. INTENSITY OF MY ANGER	1 2 3 4 5 6 7 8 9 10	1 2 3 4 5 6 7 8 9 10
6. MY BEHAVIOR AND ACTIONS		
7. THE PERSON/THING MY ANGER FOCUSED ON		
8. SELF-STATEMENTS I MADE		
9. ANGER ACTION OR RESPONSE TO SITUATION		
10. SELF-RATING MY ANGER CONTROL	1 2 3 4 5 6 7 8 9 10	1 2 3 4 5 6 7 8 9 10
11. TAKE A TIME OUT? WHAT ELSE I DID		
12. STUFF ANGER? HOW MUCH?	1 2 3 4 5 6 7 8 9 10	1 2 3 4 5 6 7 8 9 10
13. INTENSIFY MY ANGER? HOW MUCH?	1 2 3 4 5 6 7 8 9 10	1 2 3 4 5 6 7 8 9 10
14. OTHER EMOTIONS?		
15. SUBSTANCE ABUSE?		
16. PHYSICAL ACTIVITY		
17. POSITIVE SELF-TALK?		

KEY: 1 = A little 10 = A lot

Appendix B
Glossary of Relapse Prevention Terms

ABSTINENCE

A lifestyle of not acting out anger destructively, and dealing with feelings in a positive way. For people with anger problems, abstinence includes avoiding thoughts about situations that reinforce your desires to act out your anger or hurt someone, and behaviors that are associated with your anger pattern and aggressive actions (such as using alcohol and/or drugs, heated arguments, picking fights, etc.).

ABSTINENCE VIOLATION EFFECT (AVE)

The many changes in your thoughts, beliefs, and behaviors when you **lapse.** When you experience AVE, you may mistakenly conclude that you have no willpower or are unable to change. The AVE is giving up on yourself. You may think of yourself as a failure destined always to fail. You might also experience the **Problem of Immediate Gratification.** You are most likely to experience the **AVE** if you believe that you will never lapse and that you are a failure when you do lapse. But when you are prepared in advance to deal with **AVE**, your chances of reoffending are decreased.

ADAPTIVE COPING RESPONSE (ACR)

An adaptive coping response helps you avoid anger outbursts **(relapse). ACRs** are positive changes in your thoughts, feelings, and/or behaviors that help you deal with a **risk factor** or avoid a **lapse.** Adaptive coping responses may be general (such as talking it out with a friend when you are depressed or angry) or specific to certain situations (such as avoiding bars, not spending time with people who will escalate your anger, etc.).

151

General coping responses improve the quality of your life. They include managing anger and stress, improving your relationship skills, changing your lifestyle and habits so they no longer trigger your anger, learning to relax, and learning and using problem-solving skills. General adaptive coping responses help you prevent problems.

Specific coping responses deal with lapses and your personal risk factors. They include avoiding triggers to your abusive behavior (stimulus control), avoiding **risk factors,** escaping from risk factors, developing and using specific coping methods for a particular problem, changing the way you think, learning ways to reduce the impact of **AVE**, anger contracts and other methods of dealing with problems. Adaptive coping means not giving up on yourself when the going gets tough.

ANGER CONTRACT

A contract you sign with yourself or your counselor (therapist) that describes how you are going to manage your anger. Effective anger contracts include clauses that: 1) identify your anger triggers, 2) identify your **risk factors** for anger, 3) identify the cues that you are getting angry, 4) describe the **interventions** and **adaptive coping responses** you will use (i.e, time out, physical activity), 5) define the rewards you will use with yourself when you use your contract and manage your anger (i.e., getting to watch an extra hour of sports on TV, buying additional materials or supplies for your hobby, etc.), 6) describe the consequences for not using your anger contract (i.e., not watching TV, making amends or restoring damaged property, etc.), and 7) a specific time each week during which you will take time to review your anger contract.

ASSERTIVENESS

A positive way to get your needs met without aggressive actions. The ability to express your feelings in a positive, confident way.

Standing up for your rights without abusing and/or ignoring the rights of others.

COGNITIVE DISTORTION

A thinking error or irrational thought that you may use to make your anger and and acting out your anger seem OK, or to allow yourself to experience abusive emotions without attempting to change them. Basically, cognitive distortions are ways you go about justifying (or making excuses for) your acting out your anger. These thoughts distort reality.

DEFENSE MECHANISM

A way you avoid dealing with truth or reality about your anger problem. You are using defense mechanisms when you don't let the truth or reality sink in and affect your thoughts, feelings, or behavior. For example, when you rationalize, deny, minimize, or become overly intellectual about your anger and acting it out, you are using defense mechanisms.

DISINHIBITORS

Disinhibitors are generally used late in the **relapse** process to make it seem easier for you to get angry and act our your anger. Some disinhibitors are internal or inside. One kind of internal disinhibitor is a **cognitive distortion** ("he's trying to screw me over," "he's lookin' for trouble," or "she deliberately does things to piss me off.") Using alcohol and/or drugs is an example of an external disinhibitor. Disinhibitors are used to attempt to excuse aggressive or assaultive behaviors ("I wouldn't have done it if I wasn't...[drunk/ angry/lonely] at the time.").

EMPATHY

Your ability to be aware of and sensitive to the experience and feelings of another person without having them communicated explicitly. Empathy involves your ability to feel another's discomfort, pain and hurt, to see others as real human beings with feelings and as people whom you hurt.

EXTERNAL SUPERVISORY DIMENSION

The aspect of Relapse Prevention (RP) that allows significant others (employer, family, and/or friends) to monitor your anger, your **precursors** and how you are managing your anger. Its structure allows other people to understand and help you.

INTERNAL SELF-MANAGEMENT DIMENSION

The aspect of RP that allows you to better recognize and control your anger **precursors.**

INTERVENTION

The spontaneous and appropriate use of tools (thoughts and behaviors) to avoid or escape situations in which your anger is likely to be triggered or to build. Using interventions helps you prevent your anger from building.

LAPSE

An emotion, fantasy, thought, or behavior that is part of your cycle and relapse pattern. Lapses are not anger outbursts. They are **precursors** or **risk factors** for anger. Lapses are not failures and can be valuable learning experiences.

MALADAPTIVE COPING RESPONSE (MCR)

An unhelpful effort to deal with a **risk factor** or **lapse** that moves you closer to relapse. Examples: getting angry and going to a bar to relax; picking a fight with someone, etc. (many people with anger problems decide to "relax" with a drink when they're upset,

---

[3]Referred to in early RP literature and teachings as "High Risk Situations." The present term includes both external and internal stimuli.

even though they know drinking alcohol is part of their anger cycle or pattern). An MCR allows you to move from the frying pan into the fire.

PRECURSORS

A general term used to describe what happens before your anger begins to build/escalate, including: **seemingly unimportant decisions (SUDs), maladaptive coping responses (MCRs), risk factors, lapses,** and the **abstinence violation effect (AVE).**

Predisposing Precursors[4] are thoughts, feelings, and events that probably began during your childhood and still influence the way you think, feel, and behave today. One example is being physically, sexually, or emotionally abused as a child.

Precipitating Precursors[5] are thoughts, feelings, and events in your life that trigger your anger cycle and relapse process. These precursors are usually **risk factors** and triggers that show up before your acting out. Examples include arguments with others, drinking, running old tapes in your thought process, isolation, etc.

Perpetuating Precursors are thoughts, feelings, and behaviors that are generally ongoing problems in your life and often help you maintain the Pretend-Normal Phase of your anger cycle and the relapse process. Examples include unresolved anger, chronic alcohol and drug abuse, or a job with built-in high risk factors (such as working with people who feed or trigger your anger, a boss who continually picks on you or puts you down in front of others).

PROGRAMMED COPING RESPONSES

Pre-planned responses to deal constructively with specific risk factors that you might reasonably expect to encounter in the future. Rehearsing these planned coping responses maximizes your ability to manage your anger.

---

[4]Referred to in earlier RP literature as immediate precursors to sexual abuse.

[5]Referred to in earlier RP literature as early precursors to sexual abuse.

Glossary of Relapse Prevention Terms

PROBLEM OF IMMEDIATE GRATIFICATION (PIG PHENOMENON)

The **PIG** phenomenon is part of the Abstinence Violation Effect **(AVE).** It occurs when you remember only the positive sensations and relief experienced before, during, or immediately after acting out your anger. By recalling only the immediate positive sensations from past assaults you increase the likelihood that you will act out your anger again. When you experience the **PIG** phenomenon, you are more likely to forget about the negative consequences that are usually delayed (such as guilt, shame, loss of family and friends, loss of employment (and if you are arrested, publicity about your arrest and conviction, jail, parole...), etc. When you learn to counter the strength of the **PIG** phenomenon by focusing on the delayed negative effects of your actions (and the immediate and delayed harmful impact on others), you decrease your likelihood of **relapse.**

RELAPSE

Acting out your anger in a non-productive and/or destructive way.

RELAPSE PREVENTION (RP)

A process for emotional, cognitive, and behavioral self-management and external supervision of anger problems. It is the process of taking control of your life with help, support, and monitoring by your family, friends, and/or co-workers.

RISK FACTORS

Thoughts, feelings, behaviors, and situations that negatively affect your commitment to abstinence from anger outbursts and threaten your ability to maintain self-control. Risk factors lead you closer to lapses and relapses unless you intervene by using an **adaptive coping response** (ACR). Risk factors usually appear right after seemingly unimportant decisions.

SELF-DEPRECATION

Belittling or putting yourself down.

SEEMINGLY UNIMPORTANT DECISIONS (SUDs)[6]

Decisions that at first seem to have little bearing on whether a lapse or relapse will occur. **SUDs** allow you to get closer **risk factors** that increase your probability of acting out your anger. An angry person who decides to have an argument with his partner or go to the bar to have a few drinks and "relax" is making a Seemingly Unimportant Decision. In reality, arguing with a person who triggers your anger or drinking when you have a problem with alcohol (or get violent when you drink) allows you to place yourself in a high risk factor where you may **lapse** or **relapse.**

STIMULUS CONTROL

A specific coping response that removes from your daily environment all items associated with your relapse pattern. For example, if your anger cycle involves drinking or using drugs, you would want to remove all alcoholic beverages, drugs, drug paraphernalia, etc., from your home, office, and car. If being around your family triggers your anger, you would want to spend less time around them or visit them less often.

[6]Referred to in early RP literature as AIDs (Apparently Irrelevant Decisions).

Glossary of Relapse Prevention Terms

Recommended Reading

BURNS, D.
Feeling Good: The New Mood Therapy
New York: William Morrow, 1980

CHARLESWORTH, E.A., & NATHAN, R.G.
Stress Management — A Comprehensive Guide to Wellness
New York: Atheneum, 1985

CULLEN, M.
Cage Your Rage
American Correctional Association
8025 Laurel Lakes Court, Laurel, MD 20707, 1992

ELLIS, A.
The No Cop-out Therapy
Psychology Today, pp. 56-62, July 1973

GOLDSTEIN, A.P., & ROSENBAUM, A.
Aggress-Less: How to Turn Anger and Aggression into Positive Action
Englewood Cliffs, NJ: Prentice Hall, 1982

McKAY, M., ROGERS, P.D., & McKAY, J.
When Anger Hurts
Oakland, CA: New Harbinger Publications, 1989

NEIDHARDT, E.J., CONRY, R.F., & WEINSTEIN, M.S.
A Guided Self-Management Series for Stress Related Disorders
Vancouver, BC: Western Center Health Group, 1981

NOVACO, R.W.
Stress Inoculation Therapy for Anger Control
In P.A. Keller & L.G. Ritt (Eds.), 1983

Innovations in Clinical Practice: A Source Book, Vol. 2
Sarasota, FL: Professional Resource Exchange

SONKIN, D.J. & DURPHY, M.
Learning to Live Without Violence: A Handbook for Men
San Francisco, CA: Volcano Press, 1982

WEISINGER, H.D.
Dr. Weisinger's Anger Work Out Book
New York, NY: William Morrow, 1985